Who Wants to Be a
Geordie?

D1332188

Simon Newell

BLACK & WHITE PUBLISHING

First published 2004
by Black & White Publishing
99 Giles Street, Edinburgh EH6 6BZ

ISBN 1 84502 028 6

A CIP catalogue record for this book is available
from The British Library

Cover design by McCusker Graphic Media

Printed and bound by Nørhaven Paperback A/S,
Viborg Denmark

CONTENTS

INTRODUCTION

So you want to be a Geordie? But what exactly is a Geordie? This question has spurred heated debates for many, many years. Are Geordies the people of Newcastle? Or folk near the Tyne? Are Geordies Royalists? (So called because of their support for the Hanover King George I.) Or is a Geordie a Northumberland or County Durham miner? Or perhaps more simply – people who have a sticker reading 'Gan canny divvent dunsh us' on their cars.

The fact that historians don't actually have an answer to this question will fuel the debate for many generations to come. In absence of a definitive definition it may be best to ask 'Who wants to be a Geordie?' and have a number of tests which may define who's Geordier than who. The fact that some people may not wish to display this solely in terms of an appreciation of football, good humour, the ability to down 10 bottles of brown ale and follow it by a hot curry leads perhaps to a more inclusive quiz.

Who Wants to be a Geordie is a quiz book offering 500 questions which aim to separate Geordies from would-be-Geordies, pointless to some who would simply ask just one question – 'What football team do you support?' – but maybe useful all the same.

The sources of material employed in writing this book were overwhelming, and so an emphasis is placed on the area around Tyneside. I've tried to make the questions interesting and accurate and I take sole responsibility for them. I hope you enjoy the quiz.

Simon Newell
www.geordie.org.uk

ACKNOWLEDGEMENTS

I would like to thank my family, Sara, Steve Gamsby, Davey Walker and Richard for their support and suggestions. Thanks to James for his proof-reading, John and Alan for their 1970s Tyneside teenage memories. Thanks also to Campbell Brown and Penny Clarke of Black and White Publishing, for their patience and giving me the opportunity to add to an established series of books.

We are lucky that there is so much local studies literature focused on the Northeast of England. This, combined with enthusiasm of Northumbrians in creating the plethora of Northeast related web pages, is astounding and helped me immensely in compiling this book. Sites worth a mention are the Newcastle and Gateshead online Library service, Keys to the Past, David Simpson's Northeast History Pages and The Northumbrian Association.

THE QUESTIONS

1

The River

A winding line from west to east, a boundary between counties and in places, a frontier of an ancient empire, a provider of food, wealth and work – the River Tyne has undoubtedly moulded and shaped the peoples and industries which live along its length.

The North Tyne and South Tyne rivers come together to form the River Tyne in the picturesque upper Tyne Valley. The three rivers are, without doubt, an area of outstanding beauty and serve as some of Britain's finest salmon rivers.

But that wasn't always the case. During the industrial period, indiscriminate dumping of ballast, coupled with filth from the factories, made the Tyne so thick it was said that you didn't need bridges to cross it. Since the decline of industry, the river has been reclaimed by nature and in just a few decades the Tyne has again become one of Britain's best game fishing rivers.

The expression, 'Are ye frem sooth o' the watter?' is often said with distaste. This is ironic as more people in the region live south of the River Tyne than North of it – but it does refer to the natural barrier that the River forms, along with the suspicion that you may be a Mackem.

Taxi drivers are at least willing to cross the river but, despite the many river crossings, there never seem to be enough. Ferries and fords were the main methods of crossing the river until the arrival of the Romans, whose engineering skills made life a lot easier for their armies and the local populace. The river is a dangerous barrier – for example a flood in 1771 destroyed or severely damaged all river crossings except the bridge at Corbridge. The Tyne has the distinction of having the highest recorded flood flow of any river in England and Wales.

The Romans, Vikings and Angles recognised the navigational qualities of the Tyne, utilising it as part of their extensive trade routes. Keelboats, derived from Anglo-Saxon Coels, took coal to waiting colliers at the river mouth. Trade with London, the Baltic and Europe became firmly established, along with shipbuilding and fishing at North Shields.

Today, there isn't as much 'Tyne industry' and upstream, towards Newcastle and Gateshead, there isn't much river traffic – although the settlements around the Tyne are large and numerous. Maybe, in the future, the river will be used in new ways instead of just being viewed as something to cross.

1.1 How many bridges span the Tyne in Newcastle/Gateshead?

a	10	b	5
c	7	d	8

1.2 Robert Stephenson and T.E. Harrison built which bridge that spans the River Tyne?

a	Tyne Bridge	b	Swing Bridge
c	High Level Bridge	d	King George V Bridge

1.3 Which river doesn't flow into the Tyne?

a	Old Nick Waters	b	South Tyne
c	Derwent	d	Stanley Burn

1.4 A keelboat was crewed by a skipper, two keelmen and a boy. What was the boy known as?

a	A Pee Dee	b	A Bee Tree
c	The Bairn	d	A Wee Dee

1.5 Whose Oils stands on the banks of the Tyne in Gateshead?

a	Jackies	b	Harpers
c	Fenwicks	d	Bretts

1.6 What is the most recently built Tyne river crossing?

a	Gateshead Millennium Bridge	b	The Tyne Tunnel
c	Queen Elizabeth II Bridge	d	Redheugh Bridge

1.7 Which burn flows through Jesmond Dene to the Tyne?

a	Ouseburn	b	Pandon Burn
c	Lort Burn	d	Walkerburn

1.8 Who was the engineer that built the Swing Bridge?

a	Robert Stephenson	b	W.G. Armstrong
c	George Stephenson	d	Sir Thomas Bouch

1.9 When did the Metro Centre, near the banks of the Tyne, in Gateshead open?

a	1987	b	1988
c	1986	d	1989

1.10 How long is the River Tyne?

a	74 miles	b	108 miles
c	62 miles	d	96 miles

1.11 The largest vessel ever to sail along the River Tyne was called what?

a	*Mauritania*	b	*HMS Ark Royal*
c	*The Bonga*	d	*The Turbinia*

1.12 A south pier built to stop the river silting at the mouth of the River Tyne is named what?

a	Tynemouth	b	South Shields Pier
c	Marsden Pier	d	Groyne Pier

1.13 What was formed in Tynemouth in 1869?

a	First ever volunteer life brigade	b	Sea Scouts
c	Sea Cadets	d	Tynemouth Longsands Life Guard

1.14 What is the name of the floating nightclub moored near the Tyne Bridge?

a	Tuxedo Princess	b	Tuxedo Royal
c	Royal Queen	d	Royal Prince

1.15 What large monument can be seen overlooking the Tyne at Tynemouth?

a	World War I memorial	b	The High Light
c	Tynemouth Priory	d	Monument to Lord Collingwood

1.16 How long does it take for the Gateshead Millennium bridge to open or close?

a	3 mins	b	4 mins
c	1.5 mins	d	9 mins

1.17 How high is the Tyne Bridge arch at its highest point?

a	55m	b	42m
c	34m	d	65m

1.18 What was the BALTIC originally used as?

a	Paper mill	b	Fish store
c	Flour mill	d	Oil terminal

1.19 What was the name of the floating crane that brought the Gateshead Millennium Bridge up the Tyne to its present position?

a	Mercury	b	Socrates I
c	Aristotle III	d	Asian Hercules II

1.20 The meeting of the waters, the rivers North Tyne & South Tyne converge where?

a	Warden Rock	b	Acomb
c	Collerford	d	Haydon Bridge

1.21 Which two communities are connected by the Tyne Pedestrian and Cycle tunnel?

a	Wallsend & Hebburn	**b**	North Shields & Hebburn
c	Howden & Jarrow	**d**	Walker & Jarrow

1.22 Which bygone riverside community would wear a blue jacket and yellow waistcoat?

a	Keelmen	**b**	Coopers
c	Porters	**d**	Shipwrights

1.23 What is the name of the sculpture which hangs on the remains of the old Redheugh Bridge?

a	*Once upon a Tyne*	**b**	*Once upon a Time*
c	*Past Times*	**d**	*Past Tyne*

1.24 Which riverside sculpture was originally commissioned for Gateshead at the Glasgow Garden Festival 1987?

a	*Goats*	**b**	*Bottle Bank*
c	*Rolling Moon*	**d**	*Cone*

1.25 Where is the first River Tyne crossing point?

a	Kingshaw Green	**b**	Haydon Bridge
c	Ovingham	**d**	Hexham

1.26 Which Aircraft Carrier was built at Swan Hunter, Walsend and launched in 1981?

a	HMS Hermes	b	HMS Illustrious
c	HMS Ark Royal	d	HMS Invincible

1.27 What famous Roman road travels through Co. Durham from Piercebridge to Corbridge?

a	Dere Street	b	Watling Street
c	Fosse Way	d	Ermine Street

1.28 What transport link was opened on 19 October 1967?

a	Newcastle Airport	b	Tyne Tunnel
c	Newcastle Helipad	d	Lemington Bridge

1.29 In which year was the massive wooden structure, the Dunston Staithes, completed?

a	1869	b	1890
c	1908	d	1877

1.30 What was the last Navy frigate built by Swan Hunter?

a	HMS Newcastle	b	HMS Sheffield
c	HMS Glasgow	d	HMS Richmond

1.31 What, roughly, was the population of Gateshead in 1801?

a	8,500	b	16,700
c	22,000	d	31,000

1.32 What roughly was the population of Gateshead in 1901?

a	87,000	b	120,000
c	108,000	d	67,000

1.33 Which Tyne crossing, built in 1876, is in similar design, and a precursor to, the Tyne bridge?

a	Hagg Bank Bridge	b	Scotwood Bridge
c	Wylam road bridge	d	Redheugh Bridge

1.34 What happened on 6 October 1854?

a	Great fire of Newcastle and Gateshead	b	Royal Tyne Regatta
c	High Level Bridge Opening	d	Opening of Scotswood rail bridge

1.35 Who founded St Pauls Monastery at Jarrow in the seventh century?

a	St Bede	b	Benedict Biscop
c	St Cuthbert	d	St Aidan

1.36 Who was the leader of the Tyne's most notorious press gang?

a	Captain Hardyman	b	Admiral Davey
c	Lord Collingwood	d	Captain Bover

1.37 In the Discovery Museum, what is the largest ship model on display?

a	*SS Serenia*	b	*The Blenheim*
c	*HMS Chatham*	d	*HMS Telemachus*

1.38 Where near the Tyne was the Roman fort Condercum?

a	Benwell	b	Wallsend
c	Derwenthaugh	d	Ryton

1.39 How many Royal Navy vessels have borne the city of Newcastle's name?

a	5	b	12
c	2	d	8

1.40 Which port is not served by an International Ferry link from the Tyne?

a	Bergen	b	Hamburg
c	Esberg	d	Hook of Holland

1.41 The River Tyne Improvement Act ending Newcastle's monopoly of the Tyne was passed by parliament in which year?

a	1850	b	1906
c	1797	d	1820

1.42 What is the name of the latest Shields Ferry?

a	*Pride of the Tyne*	b	*The Northumbrian*
c	*The Sheildsman*	d	*Freda Cunningham*

1.43 What was the name of the ferry that this vessel replaced?

a	*Baron Newcastle*	b	*Baron Durham*
c	*Percy*	d	*Freda Cunningham*

1.44 Where on the Tyne is the pumping station designed to take water from Kielder to the Tees?

a	Riding Mill	b	Alston
c	Falstone	d	Redesmouth

1.45 In 1929, how many ferry routes operated between Newburn and the river mouth?

a	11	b	7
c	5	d	15

13

1.46 Which seventeenth-century gun battery guards the river Tyne?

a	Clifford Fort	**b**	Monks Fort
c	Shields Fort	**d**	Percy Fort

1.47 What is the world's largest square rigged sailing ship which visited the Tyne during the Tall Ships Race in 1993?

a	*Stavros S Nicarchos*	**b**	*Sedov*
c	*Prince William*	**d**	*James Cook*

1.48 What is the smallest vessel of the Tyne Leisure Line fleet?

a	*The Catherine*	**b**	*Inner Farne*
c	*The Cookson*	**d**	*Island Scene*

1.49 The Tyne Bridge and Sydney Harbour Bridge were constructed by which engineering company?

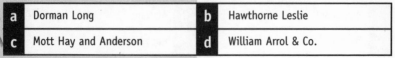

a	Dorman Long	**b**	Hawthorne Leslie
c	Mott Hay and Anderson	**d**	William Arrol & Co.

1.50 What shipping hazard lies at the foot of the Tynemouth cliffs?

a	Black Middens rocks	**b**	Herd sands
c	Tyne Bar	**d**	Priory rocks

2

The Toon and Nearby

'Newcastle had a long history as a grimy industrial powerhouse, but it has been transformed into one of the most lively and cosmopolitan cities in the country.'

University of Newcastle Upon Tyne website

Newcastle has always been known as 'The Toon.' The Toon Army are the Newcastle United fans – despite the intentions of the football club who have patented the rights to the name. Sunderland fans might insert the word 'Cart' before this name, and Toon fans would retaliate in kind.

Celtic tribes once populated the area; in fact, recent discoveries have indicated that the region was more populated in Celtic times than was originally thought, but the Romans being the clever society that they were, built a bridge and settled the site where Newcastle and Gateshead are today. Nearby, South Shields was a major port and supply base for the Roman campaigns and was operated by skilled bargemen from the River Tigris. This was hard labour and thirsty work – no wonder South Shields is where the first Working Men's Club was formed!

Benefiting from being a crossing point and having an unfair monopoly on River Tyne trade, Newcastle became a significant town. In 1334, for instance, Newcastle was the fourth wealthiest town in England, after London, Bristol and York. In 1547, Newcastle had a population of over 10,000 and included many trades and guilds. By 1730, the communities of the Tyne were exporting over 600,000 tonnes of coal and producing about 30% of the nation's glass. Development extended to centres of learning and the creation of colleges and societies like the Newcastle Mining Institute, which today houses the most comprehensive mining and mechanical engineering library in the world. New architecture in Newcastle reflected the nineteenth-century classical style with talented men creating the much admired 'City of Palaces'. Grey Street was recently voted Britain's finest street by the listeners of the BBC *Today* programme.

Today, easterly and non-America-facing Newcastle has a medium-sized population, but as a regional centre it manages to punch above its weight. Where the Luftwaffe failed, modernist leaders succeeded in flattening Georgian buildings, replacing them with projects such as the 1970s Eldon Square shopping centre, the first and largest project of its kind in Europe. Over a decade later, in Gateshead, the Metro Centre was created, which was, and is now again, Europe's largest covered shopping centre. Despite the 'progress', Newcastle still has an extremely high density of old grade I & II listed buildings in its compact city centre, making it a pleasant, photogenic place.

A recent cultural renaissance and tourism boost has seen a record number of visitors to the city. Viking hoards still come to the city, shopping instead of pillaging – record passenger numbers at its airport and ferry terminals reflect this. Despite having a high profile the population of Newcastle, like other northern towns, has declined. The challenge is to reverse this.

2.1 What is the Roman name for Newcastle upon Tyne, more specifically the fort and bridge?

| a | Segedunum | b | Vindolanda |
| c | Pons Aelius | d | Housteads |

2.2 By what other name has Newcastle been known?

| a | Brocolitia | b | Walltown |
| c | Oldcastle | d | Monkchester |

2.3 What marked the border between Newcastle and the Bishops land on Newcastle's medieval bridge?

| a | Cross of St Cuthbert | b | Archway |
| c | Blue Stone | d | Carving of a Mitre |

2.4 Which Royal granted a charter to the town of Newcastle upon Tyne confirming possession of the Town Moor?

| a | King John I | b | King Richard III |
| c | King Edward III | d | Queen Elizabeth I |

2.5 Which city in the U.S.A is linked with Newcastle upon Tyne?

| a | Tampa, Florida | b | Pittsburgh, Pennsylvania |
| c | Washington, D.C. | d | Atlanta, Georgia |

17

2.6 Which Newcastle street was allegedly the first street in the world to be lit by electricity?

a	Mosley Street	b	Grainger Street
c	Grey Street	d	Collingwood Street

2.7 What colour is the 'carpet' in front of the Laing?

a	Green	b	Blue
c	Black and White	d	Emerald

2.8 Which of the following is not a stair leading up from the Quayside?

a	Hannover Stairs	b	Long Stairs
c	Breakneck Stains	d	Crooked Stairs

2.9 What is named after Earl Grey?

a	A railway station	b	Tea
c	A bridge	d	A building

2.10 Which theatre in Newgate Street closed in 1963?

a	Empire Theatre	b	Haymarket Theatre
c	Newgate Theatre	d	Parsons Theatre

2.11 What was the department store at the corner of Market Street and Grainger Street?

a	Binns	b	Jacksons
c	Dodds	d	Doggarts

2.12 Which famous watering hole in the Haymarket was demolished to make way for Bus station improvements and Marks & Spencer's extension?

a	Percy Arms	b	The Haymarket
c	The Jubilee	d	Farmers Rest

2.13 What were public fountains in Newcastle/Gateshead called?

a	Pants	b	Spouts
c	Springs	d	Wells

2.14 Which current Newcastle church, on the site of a large medieval church, was designed by David Stephenson?

a	St Thomas the Martyre	b	St Nicholas
c	All Saints	d	St Johns

2.15 What was the name of the American clothes store that was off Westgate Road?

a	19	b	Flip
c	Yank Stores	d	West World

2.16 Which Arcade, built in 1832 and later demolished was reborn with a replica?

a	Central Arcade	b	Dobson Arcade
c	Royal Arcade	d	Handysides Arcade

2.17 Where in Newcastle will you find a Marks and Spencer 'Original Penny Bazaar'?

a	Central Arcade	b	Jesmond
c	The Haymarket	d	The Grainger Market

2.18 The first department store in Newcastle was founded by which Weardale man?

a	Emerson Muschamp Bainbridge	b	John James Fenwick
c	Amos Atkinson	d	David Dodds

2.19 Lord Armstrong donated which park to the city of Newcastle in 1883?

a	Leazes Park	b	Jesmond Dene
c	Town Moor	d	Festival Park

2.20 Where is the South African War Memorial?

a	St Nicholas place	b	Old Eldon Square
c	The Haymarket	d	Exhibition Park

2.21 In which store are there stairs with small, bent human figures supporting the handrail?

a	Fenwicks	b	Binns
c	Bainbridges	d	Co-op

2.22 In which year did the Tall Ships Race first come to Newcastle?

a	1986	b	1978
c	1983	d	1991

2.23 In which Newcastle museum would you find a mummy?

a	Hancock	b	Centre for Life
c	Antiquities	d	Discovery Museum

2.24 Where will you find Windows Music store?

a	Eldon Square	b	Central Arcade
c	Eldon Gardens	d	Monument Mall

2.25 Where does the more 'alternative' youth hang around on a Saturday afternoon?

a	The Quayside	b	High Bridge
c	Old Eldon Square	d	The Bigg Market

2.26 What transportation point was opened on 26 July 1935 at a cost of £35,000?

a	Mannors Station	b	North Shields Ferry terminal
c	Gateshead Interchange	d	Newcastle Airport

2.27 Where did Stephenson build many of the world's first locomotives, including the *Rocket*?

a	St Peters, Newcastle	b	Darlington
c	Forth Banks, Newcastle	d	Askew Road, Gateshead

2.28 Which building wasn't designed by John Dobson?

a	St Thomas the Martyr's Church	b	Central Station
c	Grainger Market	d	Theatre Royal

2.29 What is Gateshead businessman John Barras famous for?

a	Paint Manufacture	b	Brewing
c	Architecture	d	Thieving

2.30 What used to be on the site of the Newburn Business Park?

a	Power station	b	Coal staithes
c	Coble fleet	d	Soap works

2.31 Which Newcastle street is well known for its many Chinese and Cantonese restaurants?

a	Gallowgate	b	Waterloo Street
c	Low Friar Street	d	Stowell Street

2.32 What was switched 'on' on 15 January 1959?

a	Tyne Tees TV	b	Tyne Bridge lights
c	Christmas Lights – late	d	South Gosforth signal box

2.33 Which section of the Metro was first to be opened in August 1980?

a	Central Station to Whitley Bay	b	Haymarket to Tynemouth
c	Monument to Pelaw	d	Gateshead to South Gosforth

2.34 In the late thirteenth century, Newcastle was the leading English port for exporting which product?

a	Wool	b	Coal
c	Glass	d	Leather

2.35 In which years were the Northeast Coast Exhibitions held?

a	1879 & 1901	b	1881 & 1921
c	1882 & 1929	d	1892 & 1934

2.36 The later Exhibition was held on part of the town moor. Where was the original Exhibition based?

a	Saltwell Park	b	Tynemouth
c	Jesmond Dene	d	Nuns Moor

2.37 The annual fair held at Newcastle, which is said to be Europe's largest non-permanent fair, is known as what?

a	Newcastle Feast	b	The Skippings
c	The Toon Fair	d	The Hoppings

2.38 Which community lived at Sandgate?

a	Monks	b	Keelmen
c	Coopers	d	Sailers

2.39 Where in Newcastle was famous for its shoemakers and clog makers?

a	Barras Bridge	b	City Road
c	Blackett Street	d	Castle Stairs

2.40 Which building was designed by George Kenyon in the early 1950s?

a	Swan House	b	Civic Centre
c	City Library	d	Byker Wall

2.41 Where was the grand Paramount Cinema opened in 1931?

a	Newgate Street	b	Northumberland Street
c	Pilgrim Street	d	Gosforth High Street

2.42 Whose wife is buried in the cemetery of All Saints Church?

a	Earl Grey	b	Richard Grainger
c	George Orwell	d	King George III

2.43 Where in Newcastle would you find a stone rabbit with long teeth?

a	Plummer Tower, Town Walls	b	Blackfriars
c	Leazes Park	d	St Nicholas Churchyard

2.44 Who designed The Guildhall in the Newcastle Quayside, opened in 1658?

a	Robert Trollope	b	John Dobson
c	Richard Grainger	d	Thomas Oliver

2.45 Trinity House, just off Broad Chare, was home to which Guild in 1505?

a	Keelman's Guild	b	Guild of Masters and Mariners
c	Fisherman's Guild	d	Guild of Shipwrights and Riggers

2.46 Where was Paddy's Saturday Market located in Newcastle?

a	Bigg Market	b	Cloth Market
c	Milk Market	d	Haymarket

2.47 Who opened the third Redheugh Bridge in 1983?

a	Duke of Kent	b	The Queen
c	Dennis Thatcher	d	Diana, Princess of Wales

2.48 What was the former function, in 1895, of the Turnbull building, now converted to luxury apartments?

a	Printing works	b	Railway workshops
c	Poor house	d	Tobacco warehouse

2.49 John Scott, lover of Bessie Surtees and a coal fitter's son, rose to become what in politics?

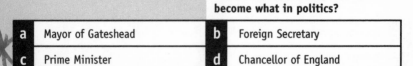

a	Mayor of Gateshead	b	Foreign Secretary
c	Prime Minister	d	Chancellor of England

2.50 Which Quayside building opened in 1877 is featured in a painting by L. S. Lowry hung in the Laing Art Gallery?

a	Sailors Bethel	b	Guildhall
c	Customs House	d	Fish Market

3

The Lingo

'Larn te taak propa leik ah dus man'

'Larn te taak propa leik ah dus man.' The dialect of the Northeast wasn't always recognised nor celebrated. Shunned by the ruling classes and the media it wasn't until fairly recently that it was heard regularly and became commonplace on national TV and Radio. This may have started in the 1960s with *The Likely Lads*, but it wasn't until serial comedy drama *Auf Weidersen Pet* in the 1980s that the masses would learn to distinguish a Geordie accent from that of Scots, Welsh or Irish. National service was a long time ago and so for many teenagers in the 1980s, it wasn't until they attended university that they became familiar with different English dialects.

The dialect differs as you travel around the region and can be referred to by many names reflecting village pride, rather than that of regional pride, dividing 'Geordie' into Tyneside, Durham, Mackem, Teesside, Northumbrian, Novocastrian, Charva and Pitmatic. It's interesting to see that today, people from outside the region recognise the term Mackem, something which would not have been the case a decade ago.

Scholars take interest in the fact that, apparently, our northern dialect is closer to Old English (Anglo-Saxon), particularly in pronunciation of vowels and retains a higher proportion of Norse-based words than that of English spoken in the south of England.

Lowland Scots is similar to Geordie, which is not surprising since the lowlands were once part of the Angle Kingdom of Northumbria. Edinburgh, being a Northumbrian town, spoke English before other parts of what is now England.

This is all very good for some, but for others it's simply 'If ya sooth o tha Rivah, ya a Mackem.' If only matters were as simple as that.

3.1 A sword with blunt edges used for performing is called a what?

a	Cleaver	b	Crowley Edge
c	Cage Call	d	Rapper

3.2 Home-made rugs made of cloth, often in mining villages in the area, are called what?

a	Miner Mats	b	Rag Rugs
c	Clippy Mats	d	Tatty Rug

3.3 Other similar rugs made in the region are called what?

a	Proggy Mats	b	Dog Rugs
c	Collier Mats	d	Tatty Rugs

3.4 What is a spuggy?

a	Sparrow	b	A go-cart
c	Pram	d	Catapult

3.5 A Mackem hails from where?

a	Gateshead	b	Sunderland
c	Middlesbrough	d	Durham

3.6 Locally, a latch on a door or gate is what?

a	Laccy	b	Bolt
c	Trammel	d	Sneck

3.7 What is a skinch?

a	A dance	b	A snack in between meals
c	A nap	d	To call a truce

3.8 Where would you find a shuggyboat?

a	The Hoppings	b	Tyne Dock
c	Saltwell Lake	d	Sweet shop

3.9 Food can be known as what?

a	Tait	b	Scrag
c	Budie	d	Scran

3.10 What is a Pit Yakkor?

a	Colliery Foreman	b	A person who washes coal
c	Not a nice term to call someone	d	Pony

3.11 What is a nettie?

a	Internet Café	b	A lavatory
c	A pie made from leftovers	d	Tool used by keelmen

3.12 What is a local word for 'friend'?

a	Mate	b	Marra
c	Buddy	d	Mucker

3.13 A burn or beck in a steep valley flows through what?

a	A Scrag	b	A Cut
c	A Wafter	d	A Dene

3.14 Where does a 'Smoggie' hail from?

a	Consett	b	Gateshead
c	Middlesbrough	d	Durham

3.15 To give someone a lift on a bike can be known as what?

a	A Hitchy	b	A Croggy
c	A Lifty	d	A Ridey

3.16 What is 'Cannae be fashed'?

a	To have no dress sense	b	Opposite to being flash
c	Can't be rude	d	Opposite to enthusiastic

3.17 What does 'Haddaway an shite!' mean?

a	Go to the lavatory	b	Never in the world
c	Please go away	d	Come on

3.18 What is something if it 'knacks'?

a	Is broken	b	Hurts
c	Clicks	d	Ryhmes

3.19 A boiler is what?

a	Is hot	b	Is extremely tough
c	Is not pleasant to the eye	d	Is heavy

3.20 What is an oxter?

a	A baby ox	b	Stock cube
c	An armpit	d	An enemy

3.21 If you have been 'plodgin', what have you been doing?

a	Digging a hole	b	Paddling in the burn
c	Assaulting the constabulary	d	Picking fruit

3.22 If a boozer is described as being stowed it is what?

a	Full	b	Closed
c	Filthy	d	Unpopular

3.23 What is 'Hoyinooteem'?

a	A winning team	b	When the pubs close
c	Spring cleaning	d	The end of a relationship

3.24 What Geordie expression describes a rainy day?

a	Belting	b	Heavily precipitating
c	Stottindoon	d	Satched

3.25 A baff weekend is what?

a	When you are skint	b	A wet weekend
c	A weekend away	d	A bad weekend

3.26 If a Geordie describes someone as 'Gitcanneyasoot' they are what?

| a | Crafty | b | Very pleasant |
| c | Incomprehensible | d | Filthy |

3.27 What is 'hoyintabs'?

| a | Throwing cigarettes | b | Something bought in a stationers |
| c | A game | d | Credit |

3.28 Where does the local word 'Gadgie' originate?

| a | Pictish | b | Friesland |
| c | Romany | d | Norwegian |

3.29 Where would you buy 'kets'?

| a | Pet shop | b | Sweet shop |
| c | Iron Monger | d | Scrap Yard |

3.30 What is a 'jumper'?

| a | Ganzie | b | Athlete |
| c | Suicidal person | d | Hare |

3.31 What is a 'workie ticket'?

a	A smug hard-working person	**b**	A pint of fine beer
c	Clocking in card	**d**	An aggravating person

3.32 What is a schooner?

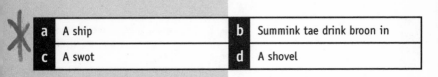

a	A ship	**b**	Summink tae drink broon in
c	A swot	**d**	A shovel

3.33 In local folklore, what is a 'worm'?

a	A dragon	**b**	Ghost
c	Serpent	**d**	Not blind

3.34 What could be known as a 'Jamie'?

a	A sandwich	**b**	A pit winding engineer
c	Lucky person	**d**	Sunderland collier

3.35 A Sand-dancer hails from where?

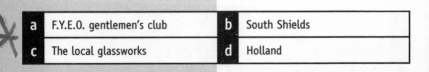

a	F.Y.E.O. gentlemen's club	**b**	South Shields
c	The local glassworks	**d**	Holland

3.36 In Geordie, what is a 'norse'?

a	Someone from Norway	b	A Viking
c	Trained medical staff	d	A code

3.37 What is a 'liggie'?

a	A catapult	b	A marble
c	A conker	d	A skittle

3.38 What other word is sometimes used?

a	Roondy	b	Penker
c	Glassy	d	Steely

3.39 What in Northumberland and Durham is a 'linn'?

a	A meadow	b	A boozer
c	Waterfall	d	A chimney

3.40 What is Geordie for 'Of course!'?

a	Hoi yee!	b	Get in!
c	Get oot!	d	Whey Aye!

3.41 Where would you find a Monkey Hanger?

a	In a wardrobe	b	In Hartlepool
c	In a shipyard	d	In a steel plant

3.42 'Wor drums' are what?

a	Are our instruments	b	Are played on a battlefield
c	Are filled with oil	d	Are packed with meats & salt

3.43 What is 'Bountie'?

a	A snack bar	b	A gangster
c	Expression for 'its bound to'	d	A ship

3.44 A 'tap on' is what?

a	Is when you get lucky	b	Is wet
c	Is at the end of the bath	d	Is a dance

3.45 What is a 'radgie gadgie'?

a	A hungry man	b	A very old man
c	A bed ridden person	d	An angry man

3.46 'Had on man' means what?

a	Please wait	b	Hold this
c	Stop thief	d	Take care

3.47 What is a 'forkeytail'?

a	A liar	b	A bird
c	An earwig	d	An aeroplane

3.48 'He's champion he is' means what?

a	That person is a champ	b	That person is a chump
c	That person is nice	d	That person is top of the class

3.49 'Would you like a cake or a meringue' would warrant a reply like what?

a	A cake please	b	A meringue please
c	How much?	d	Yes, you are correct, a cake please

3.50 Complete the sentence, 'A bogey....'

a	can be plucked with one's finger	b	has wheels
c	is a man	d	is a ghost

4

Yonks Back

Many civilisations have contributed much to the world: Romans, Greeks, Persians, Egyptians, Ottomans and Geordies. The Northumbrian region, along with others in Britain, was at the forefront of the Industrial Revolution and, at the height of its influence, was a remarkable area of intellectual development and learning.

An old school history textbook may read something like, 'First we had the Ancient Britons, Celts and then Romans. The Romans brought a great civilisation to Britain and built walls to keep out the northern barbarians. When they left, Anglo-Saxons later invaded, displacing the Britons leaving roughly what we now call England.'

We now know that this was extremely simplistic, in fact Celts were not displaced but lived and worked along side the Romans. Hadrian's Wall was not a border between England and Scotland, but in fact passes right into Newcastle, ending at the suburb Wallsend. If Roman enterprise didn't rub off on the local populous, then a tolerance for strangers did. Most of the Romans in the north came from lands that we now know as North Africa, Spain, Hungary and Romania.

When the Romans drew back to defend Rome, the locals were left to their own devices. When hassled by plundering greedy folk from outside the region, Germanic mercenaries were employed to help out. They obviously felt that life in this part of Britain was so good that they invited all their family and pals over to stay. The Angle Kingdom they created stretched from the River Forth to the River Humber. As the emerging nations of Britain started to show some semblance of present boundaries, it receded. Christianity centred on Lindisfarne and a lad called Cuthbert is celebrated as being the coolest dude who ever lived there. When Vikings invaded, his body and artefacts were taken on a Grand tour before settling for good in Durham.

The unruly north was dealt with by allowing it a degree of freedom: the Prince Bishops of Durham could raise armies, taxes and administer laws in return for allegiance to the English crown. The border was disputed for hundreds of years and for a short period of time lay partly at the River Tees. But the allegiance of the Prince Bishops to the Crown held and soldiers under the command of Bishop Bek would fight and defeat William Wallace at Falkirk. Some of the Prince Bishops' power would last till 1836 and the Palatinate Court till 1971.

The guile and inventiveness of Northumbrians perhaps evolved from all this conflict. The Reiver families of the marches and border lands lived by their own lawless rules with allegiance to their family rather than to the nation. Accepted pastime included robbery, raiding, arson, murder and extortion giving the English language such words as blackmail, bereaved, kidnap, ram-raid and twoc. Reiver family names such as Armstrong, Robson, Bell, Dixon, Milburn and Charlton are abundant in the north.

From the thirteenth century, towns such as Newcastle and Hartlepool prospered. Wealth from trading in wool and leather was surpassed by trade in coal and its related industries. The pioneering region created inventions such as steam turbines, light bulbs and passenger railways. But a downside meant that in lean periods, massive unemployment led to poor social conditions. Not that this was new to Newcastle, where in 1591, the town gave 137 licenses to beggars, twice as many as any other town, demonstrating the class gulf that always existed.

The working class communities fuelled a socialist movement, which allowed Durham to be England's first Labour controlled council. Thomas Burt, secretary of the Northumberland Miners Association was the first working man to be elected to Parliament. Lord Grey and Jack Lambton pushed the Reform Act of 1832, which gave the new industrial towns better representation in Parliament.

4.1 The son of William the Conqueror started the building which is now the present-day Castle Keep. What was he called?

a	Robert Curthose	b	Robert the Bruce
c	William Rufus	d	Malcolm Canmore

4.2 What is the barbican added to the 'New Castle' around 1250 called?

a	West Gate	b	New Gate
c	High Watch	d	The Black Gate

4.3 Newcastle became a city when the Diocese of Newcastle was formed from the Diocese of Durham. Which year was this?

a	1407	b	1643
c	1882	d	1067

4.4 Which king was prisoner in Newcastle for ten months in 1646?

a	James I	b	King Charles I
c	George III	d	George II

4.5 What was a former name for Bamburgh?

a	Gabiadini	b	Gallahad
c	Votadini	d	Din Guyardi

4.6 Which great scholar lived in the Monasteries of Monkwearmouth and Jarrow?

a	Cuthbert	b	Chad
c	Bede	d	Aiden

4.7 In which year was Gateshead annexed for two years to Newcastle?

a	1604	b	1553
c	1686	d	1776

4.8 Which regiment raised 51 battalions during the Great War, more than any other?

a	The Durham Light Infantry	b	The Northumberland Fusiliers
c	The Black Watch	d	The Green Howards

4.9 What is the Monastery at Jarrow called?

a	St Cuthberts	b	St Peters
c	St Marks	d	St Pauls

4.10 What were the Roman fort remains located at modern day South Shields called?

a	Arbeia	b	Concangium
c	Housesteads	d	Vindolanda

4.11 By what other name was Hadrian's Wall known?

a	Scots Wall	b	Pictish Wall
c	Antonine Wall	d	Empire Wall

4.12 How long in modern miles is Hadrian's Wall?

a	102	b	73
c	82	d	89

4.13 Which town was home to Tyneside's fishwives?

a	Cullercoates	b	North Shields
c	Whitley Bay	d	Hebburn

4.14 The north's *Doomsday Book* is called what?

a	*The Cuthbert Book*	b	*The Durham Book*
c	*The Boldon Book*	d	*The Pudsey Book*

4.15 Which town was known as 'Little Moscow' in the 1920s?

a	Jarrow	b	Chopwell
c	Birtley	d	Blaydon

4.16 Which Tyneside town had, at the height of its trade, over 200 salt pans?

a	Wallsend	b	Felling
c	South Shields	d	Seaton Burn

4.17 The region's first colliery railways were known as what?

a	Newcastle Roads	b	Shildon Waggonways
c	Darlington Lines	d	Wylam Tramways

4.18 Which railway claims to be the world's oldest existing railway?

a	Wylam Waggonway	b	The Bowes Railway
c	The Whickham Grand Lease Way	d	The Tanfield Railway

4.19 Who founded the monastery at Lindisfarne?

a	Cuthbert	b	Aiden
c	Oswald	d	Bede

4.20 What treasure dedicated to St Cuthbert is now kept at the British Library London?

a	*The Lindisfarne Gospels*	b	*The Durham Gospels*
c	*The Book of Kells*	d	*Codex Amiatinus*

4.21 In which year was this treasure taken from the Cathedral at Durham?

a	1610	b	1405
c	1539	d	1635

4.22 Which Celtic tribe settled around the Tyne and nearby?

a	Parisi	b	Votadini
c	Carvetti	d	Brigantes

4.23 What was the name of the Angle Kingdom north of the River Tees?

a	Deira	b	Northumbria
c	Lindsey	d	Bernicia

4.24 What Celtic river name means 'Oak River'?

a	Derwent	b	Tyne
c	Wear	d	Team

4.25 People in Co. Durham were sometimes known as what?

a	Pilgrims	b	Dunholmers
c	Oxen	d	Haliwerfolk

45

4.26 Which unpopular Bishop of Durham was slain at Gateshead in 1081?

a	Bishop Antony Bek	**b**	Bishop Thomas Hatfield
c	Bishop William Walcher of Loraine	**d**	Bishop Robert Comine

4.27 Where in Newcastle were the Northumberland Assizes once kept?

a	The Moot Hall	**b**	St Nicholas Cathedral
c	Guildhall	**d**	Castle Keep

4.28 What Tyneside village was the site of a Civil War battle in 1644?

a	Corbridge	**b**	Newburn on Tyne
c	North Shields	**d**	Dunston

4.29 Which castle is known as the Windsor of the North?

a	Raby	**b**	Barnard
c	Alnwick	**d**	Dustanburgh

4.30 In which year was Saltwell Park opened?

a	1912	**b**	1922
c	1790	**d**	1876

4.31 William Wailes, who built Saltwell Towers, was famous for what?

a	Ceramics	b	Stained glass
c	Landscape gardening	d	Printing

4.32 Where did sword makers from Soligen, Germany settle around the year 1690?

a	Ebchester	b	Shotley Bridge
c	Whickham	d	Rowlands Gill

4.33 Which Northumbrian king founded the monastery at Tynemouth in 637?

a	Edwin	b	Aethelfrith
c	Eanfrith	d	Oswald

4.34 Which Scottish king is buried at Tynemouth Monastery?

a	Kenneth Macalpin	b	Donald Ban
c	Malcolm Canmore	d	Duncan I

4.35 What is the name of the old beacon, between Wreckenton and Windy Nook?

a	Windmill Beacon	b	Beacon Lough
c	Bishops Beacon	d	North Durham Beacon

4.36 By what other Northeast name is the Eider Duck known as?

| a | Durham Duck | b | Cuddy Duck |
| c | Farne Duck | d | Sitting Duck |

4.37 Which Newcastle building houses The North of England Institute of Mining and Mechanical Engineers?

| a | Saville Hall | b | Neville Hall |
| c | Londonderry Hall | d | Bolbec Hall |

4.38 Who, in 1831, objected to Gateshead being represented in Parliament?

| a | Marquis of Londonderry | b | Lord Lambton |
| c | Bishop of Durham | d | Lord Percy |

4.39 William Hedley is best remembered for two engines. Puffing Billy was one, what was the other?

| a | Hauling Harry | b | Chuffing Silly |
| c | Wylam Dilly | d | Waggon Way Willy |

4.40 Which newspaper is now the UK's oldest provincial evening newspaper?

| a | South Shields Gazette | b | Northumberland Gazette |
| c | Sunderland Echo | d | Evening Chronicle |

4.41 Which Northumbrian king perhaps inspired the name of the city of Edinburgh?

a	Ecgfrith	b	Eadfrith
c	Edwin	d	Oswald

4.42 Which famous tea company, with premises in many Northeast towns, established a head office in Byker in 1926?

a	Nambarrie Tea Company	b	Ringtons Tea
c	Pearson Tea	d	Co-op

4.43 From where to where, did Stephenson's Locomotives operate the world's first passenger railway?

a	Shildon to Stockton	b	Darlington to Stockton
c	Darlington to Middlesbrough	d	High Etherly to Darlington

4.44 The first lighthouse in the world to be powered by electricity is at Whitburn. What is it called?

a	St Mary's	b	Roker Lighthouse
c	Souter Lighthouse	d	Longstone Lighthouse

4.45 What is the world's oldest railway bridge?

a	Causey Arch	b	The High Level Bridge
c	Dunston Staithes	d	Bowes Bridge

4.46 Who is Northumberland's, and Britain's, most famous landscape gardener?

a	William Andrews Nesfield	b	Lancelot 'Capability' Brown
c	Lord Cobham	d	Sir William Lorraine

4.47 Which battle probably established the Tweed as the border between Northumberland and Scotland, rather than Edinburgh?

a	Flodden (1513)	b	Humbleton Hill (1402)
c	Carham (1018)	d	Otterburn (1388)

4.48 Which battle is known in ballads as the Battle of Chevy Chase?

a	Flodden (1513)	b	Halidon Hill (1333)
c	Alnwick (1093)	d	Otterburn (1388)

4.49 The Northumbrian flag is based upon whose banner?

a	St Oswald	b	St Cuthbert
c	Penda	d	Edwin

4.50 Which Northeast coastal town is said to still be at war with Russia?

a	Hartlepool	b	Berwick
c	Whitby	d	Seaham

5

Culcha and Tha

'a piece of public art unique in the history of this country, and in time I think it may only compare with the Eiffel Tower and the Statue of Liberty.'

Lord Gowrie on
The Angel of the North

Geordie's and culture, in the same sentence? The bumbling antics of Geordies on television do not portray a region which gave learning, chronicles and language to the world. The magnificent book dedicated in honour to St Cuthbert is testament to this.

It wasn't always a bed of roses. Like most things in our region, when they get recognition they get pillaged. Our footballers, like Beardsley, Waddle and Gazza were nicked and magnificent books representing a scholastic and unified region were nicked. To see the *Lindisfarne Gospels* you have to visit the rather uninspiring British Library next to St Pancras Station in London.

Northumbrian culture is displayed in various guises. Songs, ballads and music performed by tartan clad Northumbrian pipers, Durham clog and sword dancing to the brass bands which parade during the Durham Big Meet and Northumberland miner's picnics. Daft lads in a Northumberland village do their bit by parading on New Year's Eve carrying blazing tar barrels above their heads – thankfully no one expects the rest of us to go to that extreme. Modern-day recordings and publications include a host of well-known singers, artists, novels and *Viz*.

Awareness of Northumbrian culture is perhaps greater now than it has been for many years and its growth is gathering pace. There is a mammoth amount of popular songs, prose and poetry from famous bards to dialect-inspired verse by local pitman. Some of this is commonly known and often sung, the forgotten being remembered and chronicled in impressive online lottery-funded projects. A huge new music centre on the banks of the Tyne will be home, not only to an orchestra, but also to a folk organisation.

The growth hasn't gone unnoticed by commercial leaders, and today, culture is a big sell. For some this simply means, erect a gallery and surround it with businesses, expensive apartments and hotels. Newcastle has lost countless small and medium-sized live music venues in the last fifteen years. These, thankfully, seem to be on the rise again. There is no denying that a culture-inspired renaissance is happening: the massive statue which greets travellers on the A1 is embraced and the symbol of the angel is used region wide on logos, on T-shirts and in names of hotels and guesthouses. It even wore a huge Newcastle United shirt to celebrate an FA cup final – but some moaner passing in his car complained and killjoy authorities forced the fans to take it down, after just 20 minutes. Why I don't know. If its massive wingspan is embracing the region then surely football is part of its embrace?

5.1 Who wrote the famous Tyneside song 'The Blaydon Races'?

a	Harry Clasper	b	John Balambra
c	Geordie Ridley	d	Joseph Armstrong

5.2 Who is the big and bonnie lass who likes beer?

a	Bessie Surtees	b	Cushie Butterfield
c	Alice Ridley	d	Aunt Ticketty

5.3 Which poet, born at Battle Hill, Hexham, wrote a volume of war poetry entitled *Battle*?

a	Sid Chaplin	b	Fred Reed
c	Algernon Swinburne	d	Wilfrid Gibson

5.4 Which North Shields author wrote *The Machine Gunners* and *Fathom Five*?

a	Robert Westall	b	Reginald Hill
c	Christopher Goulding	d	Jack Common

5.5 Which Newcastle Theatre housed playwrights Lee Hall, Julia Darling and Alan Plater?

a	Newcastle Playhouse	b	Live Theatre
c	Theatre Royal	d	The People's Theatre

5.6 What is the founding name of the Newcastle People's Theatre?

a	Clarion Dramatic Club	b	Socialist Party Arts Society
c	Percy Drama Club	d	Leazes Park Dramatics Group

5.7 Which famous dramatist and socialist performed and made his last public speech at The People's Theatre?

a	George Bernard Shaw	b	Harold Pinter
c	J.B. Priestley	d	John Whiting

5.8 In the Blaydon Races, which bridge was crossed when the bus headed into Blaydon Town?

a	Scotswood bridge	b	Blaydon Bridge
c	Chain Bridge	d	Newburn Bridge

5.9 A statue of whom stands in North Shields?

a	Charlie Chaplin	b	Norman Wisdom
c	Scott Dobson	d	Stan Laurel

5.10 The 'little waster' was more commonly known as what?

a	Billy Martin	b	Dick Irwin
c	Bobby Thompson	d	Norman Wisdom

5.11 Which singer and songwriter with the band Lindisfarne died in 1999?

a	Alan Price	b	Rod Clemments
c	Alan Hull	d	Ray Jackson

5.12 What is the local folk song commemorating a railway journey from Rowland's Gill called?

a	'Wor Nanny's a Mazer'	b	'Keep your feet still Geordie Hinny'
c	'The Waggoner'	d	'Geordies lost his liggy'

5.13 Paddy McAloon from Witton Gilbert founded which popular band?

a	Prefab Sprout	b	Geordie
c	Gangsters of Ska	d	Toy Dolls

5.14 To which country did Lambton go to in folklore and the song 'The Lambton Worm'?

a	Israel	b	Ceylon
c	Palestine	d	Persia

5.15 Which 1960s Newcastle band was formed by Alan Price?

a	Lindisfarne	b	Geordie
c	The Animals	d	Brethren

5.16 Which Beatles song was written in a Newcastle hotel and went on to become a massive selling disc?

a	'Help'	b	'She Loves You'
c	'Hey Jude'	d	'Day Tripper'

5.17 Which hotel was this?

a	Imperial Hotel	b	Royal Station Hotel
c	Turks Head Hotel	d	Caledonian Hotel

5.18 What folk organisation is based at the new Sage music centre in Gateshead?

a	High Level Ranters	b	Folkworks
c	The Northern Sinfonia	d	FARNE

5.19 What children's TV entertainment programme was based in Tynemouth in the 1980s?

a	Geordie Racer	b	Byker Grove
c	Jockies Giants	d	Supergran

5.20 Which feature film staring Michael Caine was shot in and around Newcastle in 1971?

a	Get Carter	b	The Clouded Yellow
c	Payroll	d	Jack's Return Home

5.21 Who was the author of the book which inspired this film?

a	Derek Bickerton	**b**	Christopher Goulding
c	Mike Hodges	**d**	Ted Lewis

5.22 What's the name of the film set in Newcastle that stars Patsy Kensit?

a	*Stormy Monday*	**b**	*Purely Belter*
c	*The One and Only*	**d**	*Billy Elliot*

5.23 Cecil McGivern introduced which programme to regional BBC radio?

a	*Newcastle 5NO*	**b**	*Wot Cheor Geordie*
c	*Stag-Shaw Looks Forward*	**d**	*The People's Show*

5.24 Which Co. Durham born author writes the children's Horrible Histories?

a	Christopher Goulding	**b**	Anne Wood
c	Reginald Hill	**d**	Terry Deary

5.25 Which Northumberland village celebrates New Year with a procession of flaming tar barrels?

a	Alston	**b**	Allenheads
c	Allendale Town	**d**	Blanchland

5.26 Who did the BBC poach from Tyne Tees in 1964?

a	New Bridge Street studios	**b**	Adrian Cairns
c	Bill Steel	**d**	Mike Neville

5.27 Who was the cousin of Cushie Butterfield?

a	Paddy Fagan	**b**	Tom Gray
c	Joe Wilson	**d**	Bob Johnson

5.28 What is the third fish that Little Jacky will have when the boat comes in?

a	Salmon	**b**	Haddock
c	Mackerel	**d**	Bloater

5.29 In what year did the Newcastle City Hall open?

a	1927	**b**	1934
c	1939	**d**	1947

5.30 What was the first book to be published by Catherine Cookson?

a	*The Fifteen Streets*	**b**	*The Mallen Girl*
c	*Kate Hannigan*	**d**	*The Black Candle*

5.31 Which famous engraver had workshops behind St Nicholas Cathedral and was a master and business partner of Thomas Bewick?

a	Ralph Collard	b	William Harvey
c	William Blake	d	Ralph Beilby

5.32 What was the first story to be published by Sidney Chaplin, while he was working as a miner in Co. Durham?

a	*My Fate Cries Out*	b	*The Thin Seam*
c	*The Leaping Lad*	d	*The Day of the Sardine*

5.33 Which town is the current home of the Northumbrian Bagpipe Museum?

a	Alnwick	b	Morpeth
c	Bamburgh	d	Wooler

5.34 Which song did Robson Green and Jerome Flynn reach No. 1 with in the UK singles charts?

a	'Up on the Roof'	b	'Sealed with a Kiss'
c	'Don't Stop'	d	'Unchained Melody'

5.35 Who was perhaps the most famous Northumbrian poet of the nineteenth century?

a	Algernon Swinburne	b	Percy Shelley
c	William Morris	d	Sid Chaplin

5.36 Which of the Romantic painters was born in Haydon Bridge?

a	J.W.M. Turner	b	John Martin
c	John Constable	d	Theodore Geriault

5.37 In which Shakespeare play does the Earl of Northumberland, Harry Hotspur appear in a major role?

a	*Richard III*	b	*Henry IV Part 1*
c	*Henry V*	d	*Richard II*

5.38 Which Mercury Music nominee based in Newcastle had a debut album called *Dog Leap Stairs*?

a	Kathryn Tickell	b	Beth Orten
c	Kathryn Williams	d	Kate Rusby

5.39 Who wrote the music for 'Close The Coalhouse Door'?

a	Mike Harding	b	Bob Fox
c	Alex Glasgow	d	Ed Pickford

5.40 Which famous American maritime painter lived for nearly two years in Cullercoats?

a	Winslow Homer	b	Charles Brooking
c	Robert Salmon	d	James Hamilton

5.41 Who stars as Kate Tyler in Eastenders?

a	Kim Medcalf	b	Charlie Brooks
c	Michelle Ryan	d	Jill Halfpenny

5.42 Which famous film director was born in South Shields in 1937?

a	Terry Jones	b	Danny Boyle
c	Sir Alfred Hitchcock	d	Ridley Scott

5.43 Who was a famous and popular Polish dwarf entertainer, 3ft 3ins high, who loved Durham and retired there in 1791?

a	Joseph Boruwlaski	b	Countess Humiecka
c	Bebe	d	Thorin Oakensheild

5.44 Which Gosforth-born actor read electrical engineering at Newcastle University?

a	Phil Cool	b	Rowan Atkinson
c	Michael Hodgson	d	Robson Green

5.45 Which songwriter composed music for the stage show of *Billy Elliot*?

a	Sir Cliff Richard	b	Richard O'Brien
c	Sir Elton John	d	Sir Andrew Lloyd Webber

5.46 Who produced *Roger's Profanisaurus*?

a	Roget's American Press	b	Oxford University Press
c	Collins Press	d	Roger Mellie

5.47 Who has silver buckles on his knee?

a	Tommy Armstrong	b	Bobby Shaftoe
c	The Bonny Pit Laddie	d	Young Lambton

5.48 Which sculptor created *The Angel of the North*?

a	Amish Kapoor	b	Anthony Gormley
c	Martin Puryear	d	William Pye

5.49 Which popular music show in the 1980s was filmed at the Newcastle Tyne Tees television studios?

a	*The Roxy*	b	*The Old Grey Whistle Test*
c	*The Tube*	d	*The White Room*

5.50 Where is the home of Northern Stage?

a	Newcastle Playhouse	b	The Live Theatre
c	The People's Theatre	d	The Arts Centre

6
Footie

'Some people tell me that we professional players are soccer slaves. Well, if this is slavery, give me a life sentence.'

Sir Bobby Charlton

The Northeast of England has always been a hot bed of football, along with the other renowned areas such as Liverpool, Manchester and Glasgow. So many talented footballers came from the region to play and manage clubs around Britain that it was once said that you only had to shout down a mine shaft to get a decent team. How they were suddenly allowed to down tools and start playing football is anyone's guess and there is only one surviving colliery now, so maybe that's why, in terms of cups and medals, the big three Northeast football teams have won next to nowt in the past 30 years. It's amazing how the teams can command large crowds despite modest populations and bare trophy rooms.

The fierce rivalry between Newcastle and Sunderland is well known and it's believed the earliest recording of a tussle between football supporters was over a Newcastle and Sunderland fixture in 1901. What is little known is that the rivalry is not only football related and possibly dates back to the time of the English Civil War. The displays of violence are probably nothing compared to the original football games in which whole villages would kick a pig's bladder around for a whole day. Sedgefield and Alnwick claim to have started the game.

Football isn't just focussed on the professional clubs, the Northern League is the second oldest league in the world after the Football League. Famous Northeast semi-pro teams that still play regular football are Bishop Auckland, Spennymoor United, Crook Town, Blyth Spartans, Ashington and Bedlington Terriers. Kick off for the Northern League used to be 3:15 on a Saturday, so that the lads could finish their pints in drinking up time before taking to the field.

Whether you're a bairn or a granny, football is prominent in many conversations. Work on a Monday morning starts slowly as colleagues discuss and dissect the weekend's games with renewed rivalry. Heroes in life are drawn from deep interest and local football icons grace the walls of many a house in the region. If a footballer is successful, legendary status is ensured. 'Wor Jackie', the world's most modest footballer is testament to this and he is well known by all generations to this day.

The inclusion of lots of teams under the umbrella of 'Northeast' is probably due to the fact that some are extremely isolated. Carlisle, for instance, is England's most remote football ground and is featured in the Northeast press. Berwick Rangers is featured too, except that they play in Scottish football. Gretna, a Scottish club that used to be in the Northern League, also now play in the Scottish leagues.

6.1 The highest league position attained by South Shields FC was sixth in the old second division. What season was this?

a	1929–1930	b	1921–1922
c	1926–1927	d	1934–1935

6.2 From which team did Newcastle sign Mirandinha?

a	Palmeiras	b	Santos
c	Sao Paulo	d	Fluminense

6.3 Which County Durham club won the 'World Cup' in 1909 and 1911?

a	Bishop Auckland	b	West Auckland
c	Shildon	d	Crook Town

6.4 Which team did they beat?

a	Real Madrid	b	Inter Milan
c	Athletico Madrid	d	Juventus

6.5 In which year was the Northern League formed?

a	1889	b	1879
c	1882	d	1892

6.6 Who won the first Northern League championship?

a	St Augustine's Darlington	b	Middlesbrough Ironopolis
c	Ferryhill Athletic AFC	d	Sunderland A

6.7 Blyth Spartans played in the FA Cup 5th round replay in 1978 against which team?

a	Swansea	b	Wrexham
c	Tranmere Rovers	d	Chester City

6.8 Who did Gateshead AFC beat in the FA Cup 3rd round in 1953 before reaching the quarter-final stage?

a	Preston North End	b	Liverpool
c	Tranmere Rovers	d	Blackburn Rovers

6.9 What is the nickname of Berwick Rangers FC?

a	The Sassenachs	b	The Cuddies
c	The Borderers	d	The Reivers

6.10 A good Sunderland AFC team in the early 1900s were known as what?

a	Cock of the North	b	Team of all Talents
c	Great Northern	d	Wear Wonders

6.11 Which three years in the 1950s did Newcastle United win the FA Cup?

a	1950, 1952, 1956	b	1951, 1952, 1955
c	1952, 1953, 1956	d	1951, 1953, 1955

6.12 Where was Sunderland AFC's first football ground?

a	Heratio Street	b	Groves Field, Ashbrook
c	Newcastle Road	d	Blue House Field, Hendon

6.13 In what year did Newcastle United claim their first FA cup victory?

a	1907	b	1910
c	1908	d	1913

6.14 Who was Newcastle's first 'manager'?

a	Stan Seymour	b	Charlie Mitten
c	Andy Cunningham	d	Colin Veitch

6.15 Who was the opposition in Newcastle United's first FA Cup victory?

a	Sunderland	b	Everton
c	Barnsley	d	Stoke City

6.16 Which team did Newcastle United play when they recorded their highest attendance of 68,386?

a	Manchester United	b	Sunderland
c	Chelsea	d	Liverpool

6.17 Newcastle United's record league victory was against Newport County in 1946. What was the score?

a	9-0	b	10-2
c	15-0	d	13-0

6.18 For Newcastle United, who holds the record of most league and cup goals in one season?

a	Jackie Milburn	b	Hughie Gallacher
c	Mick Quinn	d	Andy Cole

6.19 When Newcastle United beat Royal Antwerp in the UEFA cup in 1994 what was the aggregate score?

a	7-2	b	6-3
c	9-1	d	10-2

6.20 On 23 October 1986, which other team played at 'home' at Hartlepool's Victoria ground?

a	Middlesbrough	b	Darlington
c	Guisborough Town	d	Billingham Sinfonia

6.21 Who was the Newcastle United captain who lifted the Inter City Fairs cup in 1969?

a	Bobby Moncur	b	Joe Harvey
c	Wyn Davies	d	Tony Green

6.22 Which team did Newcastle United beat in the semi-final of their Fairs Cup run in 1969?

a	Inter Milan	b	FC Brugge
c	Anderlect	d	Glasgow Rangers

6.23 Which goalkeeper of the Fairs Cup winning team of 1969 went on to manage the club in later years?

a	Jim Smith	b	Bill McGarry
c	Willie McFaul	d	Gordon Lee

6.24 Who did Newcastle United draw in the 5th round of their 1973/1974 FA Cup run?

a	West Bromwich Albion	b	Nottingham Forrest
c	Scunthorpe	d	Derby County

6.25 In the 1966 World Cup, which team did not play at Ayresome Park?

a	South Korea	b	Italy
c	USSR	d	Chile

6.26 Who gives himself credit for the breaking of Newcastle's London Hoodoo in 2001?

a	Alan Shearer	b	Andy O'Brien
c	Graham Poll	d	Uri Geller

6.27 What was a previous nickname of Sunderland FC?

a	The Rokerites	b	The Reds
c	The Mackems	d	The Roker Roar

6.28 In which year did Middlesbrough FC win the FA Cup?

a	1926	b	1939
c	1938	d	1949

6.29 Who were Darlington's first opponents when they reached the 2nd division for the first time?

a	Nottingham Forrest	b	Grimsby Town
c	Derby County	d	Chesterfield

6.30 Which Northeast football team doesn't play in black and white stripes?

a	Ashington	b	Spennymoor United
c	Billingham Synthonia	d	Newcastle United

6.31 In 1908 Sunderland beat Newcastle 9-1. What else happened that season?

a	Newcastle won the FA cup	b	Newcastle won the league
c	There was a riot	d	Sunderland won the FA cup

6.32 How many times were Gateshead put up for re-election before losing their place in the Football League?

a	1	b	3
c	4	d	5

6.33 On 18 April 1903 Sunderland won a league match against Middlesbrough, what was unique about the game?

a	Game was at St James' Park	b	Sunderland fielded 11 non-English players
c	Sunderland played in black and white	d	Sunderland had a record crowd

6.34 Who were Newcastle United's opponents for Len Shackleton's debut?

a	Stockport County	b	Derby County
c	Newport County	d	Nottingham Forrest

6.35 How many goals did he score?

a	7	b	5
c	6	d	3

6.36 Who did Newcastle United play in the 6-6 thriller ZDS Cup tie in 1991?

a	Mansfield Town	b	Tranmere Rovers
c	Oldham Athletic	d	Bolton Wanderers

6.37 What colour star is Seaham?

a	Blue	b	Red
c	White	d	Green

6.38 Which past Newcastle United player 'Gets the ball, and scores a goal'?

a	Andy Hunt	b	Peter Withe
c	Alan Shoulder	d	Andy Cole

6.39 Which successful Sunderland manager in the 1890s later moved on to establish Liverpool as a force?

a	William McGregor	b	Alan Brown
c	Tom Watson	d	James Allan

6.40 Sunderland Football Club enjoyed top flight football from 1890 till which year?

a	1958	b	1964
c	1952	d	1967

72

6.41 Where do Carlisle United play?

a	Glasgow Road	b	Burndon Park
c	Cumberland Park	d	Brunton Park

6.42 What was the name of the 'World' cup that West Auckland won twice?

a	Sir Thomas Lipton Cup	b	Jules Rimet Trophy
c	The World Club Cup	d	The World Cup

6.43 Who was known as 'Mr Newcastle'?

a	Joe Harvey	b	Stan Seymour
c	Jackie Milburn	d	Tom Watson

6.44 Who were the last team to visit Ayresome Park in a competitive game?

a	Cambridge United	b	Burnley
c	Luton Town	d	Port Vale

6.45 Which famous football stadium architect designed stands at Roker Park?

a	Alexander Blair	b	Derek Wilson
c	Sir John Simpson	d	Archibald Leitch

6.46 When St James' Park lost out as a venue for the 1966 World Cup, which ground hosted the stage matches instead?

a	Ayresome Park	b	Elland Road
c	Goodison Park	d	Ibrox

6.47 Who scored the vital goal at St James' Park against Portsmouth at the end of the 1991/1992 season?

a	Andy Hunt	b	Lee Clark
c	David Kelly	d	Gavin Peacock

6.48 Which team stopped Newcastle United's record unbeaten run at the start of the 1992/1993 promotion season?

a	Grimsby Town	b	Luton Town
c	Swindon Town	d	Mansfield Town

6.49 Which team did not play at St James' Park in Euro '96?

a	France	b	Romania
c	Bulgaria	d	Belgium

6.50 In Newcastle United's first Champions League campaign, which team was not part of the group?

a	Barcelona	b	Croatia Zagreb
c	Dynamo Kiev	d	PSV Eindhoven

7

Other Sport

Some people may never believe it, but in the Northeast there is indeed sport other than football. This isn't incidentally racing whippets, pigeons, playing dominoes, snooker and darts. Although football commands matters, the region has produced some top class athletics, cricket, ice hockey, rugby and . . . darts teams. However, the domineering factor of football allegiance does influence, for example, some Durham cricket fans wear cricket jerseys with either a small Newcastle badge or Sunderland badge.

Despite vicious winds from the North Sea and rain like bullets, water sports are very popular. Who would have thought that a Northeast beach would become a regular venue for the British National Surf Cup championships or that our rivers would become so clean that people can spend leisurely weekends jet skiing along the Tyne or white water rafting at the Tees barrage.

Gateshead International Stadium has hosted great athletic meetings where athletes have produced some outstanding world records. In Durham folklore it is said that people in the county make good athletes because in days long ago, they had to run away from wild boar who roamed the road west of Durham city giving the name to the village of Brancepeth.

Rowing was a massive working class spectator sport, the regatta at Durham pre-dates Henley and the sport in its heyday produced some huge heroes. Indeed, when the Tyne's most famous rowing son Harry Clasper competed, crowds of 80,000 to 100,000 would line the banks of the river. When he died, an estimated 130,000 people lined the route of the funeral. Fittingly, the way was so congested that part of the procession had to be by barge on the river, as it led to his final resting place in Whickham.

7.1 What was the previous name of The Newcastle Falcons Rugby Club?

a	Gosforth	b	Kenton
c	Newcastle Rangers	d	Newcastle Hawks

7.2 What were the original colours of the above team?

a	Purple	b	Green and yellow hoops
c	Green and black hoops	d	Green and white hoops

7.3 In which ground do the rugby team play?

a	St James' Park	b	Gosforth Park
c	Kingston Park	d	Leazes Park

7.4 What was the name of the Newcastle Arena's first ice hockey team?

a	Newcastle Cobras	b	Newcastle Vipers
c	Newcastle Eagles	d	Newcastle Warriors

7.5 In which year did Gosforth first win the John Player cup?

a	1958	b	1967
c	1976	d	1982

7.6 What annual sport was re-instated in Newcastle in 1997?

a	Speedway	b	Rowing
c	Coits	d	Ice Hockey

7.7 From which team did the Newcastle Cobras originate?

a	Durham Wasps	b	Sunderland Chiefs
c	Billingham Bombers	d	Whitley Warriers

7.8 Which famous and successful boat was built by Harry Clasper?

a	*The Lord Boyne*	b	*The Lord Ravensworth*
c	*Duke of Northumberland*	d	*Lord Armstrong*

7.9 In what year did Harry Clasper compete in his last rowing race?

a	1870	b	1862
c	1867	d	1906

7.10 In what year was the inaugural Tyne Regatta?

a	1795	b	1840
c	1815	d	1901

7.11 How many gold medals at Commonwealth, World and European games has Steve Cram won during his career?

a	6	b	10
c	3	d	5

7.12 Where was Tyneside's first ever dirt track race, later to become Speedway?

a	Gosforth Park, Gosforth	b	Felling
c	Brough Park, Byker	d	Hillheads, Whitley Bay

7.13 What was formed on 4 June 1892 in the Lockharts Cocoa Rooms, Clayton Street, Newcastle?

a	Newcastle United Football Club	b	Newcastle United Workmen's Golf Club
c	Felling Flyfishing Club	d	Newcastle Chess Club

7.14 What is the capacity for sport in the Newcastle Arena?

a	5500	b	7500
c	3500	d	10000

7.15 What was the name of Gateshead's professional Rugby League side awarded a franchise in 1999?

a	Storm	b	Tornado
c	Thunder	d	Hurricane

7.16 Which Rugby League side bought the Gateshead outfit after just one season?

a	Bradford Bulls	b	Wakefield
c	Leeds Rhinos	d	Hull Sharks

7.17 Which team did England play in Jonny Wilkinson's debut in April 1988?

a	South Africa	b	Australia
c	Ireland	d	Scotland

7.18 Which is the region's oldest and the UK's fourth oldest golf club?

a	Alnmouth	b	Bellingham
c	Durham	d	Wrekenton

7.19 Who established the Great North Run?

a	Steve Ovet	b	Steve Cram
c	Brendan Foster	d	Sebastian Coe

7.20 In which year did Durham C.C.C. gain first class cricket?

a	1994	b	1989
c	1986	d	1991

7.21 Which of the following was not a famous Tyne oarsman of the nineteenth century?

a	James Renforth	b	Harry Clasper
c	Robert Chambers	d	Robert Coombes

7.22 In which event did Steve Cram compete and win a Silver medal in in the 1984 Olympics?

a	800m	b	1500m
c	Steeplechase	d	5000m

7.23 Which club did Brendan Foster and Steve Cram both compete for?

a	Blaydon Harriers	b	Gateshead Harriers
c	Morpeth Harriers	d	South Tyneside Harriers

7.24 What event did Brendan Foster compete and win a bronze medal in, in the 1976 Olympics?

a	1500m	b	5000m
c	800m	d	10000m

7.25 Which is the Northeast's oldest established athletics club?

a	Morpeth	b	Durham City
c	Gateshead	d	Elswick

7.26 From which Northeast town is Chris Newton, bronze Olympian and Great Britain cycling team member from?

a	Cramlington	b	Stockton on Tees
c	Consett	d	Hartlepool

7.27 What is the motor racing venue just south of Darlington?

a	Catterick	b	Richmond
c	Croft	d	Middleton St George

7.28 In which event did Olympian Jonathan Edwards win a gold medal in 2000, and a silver medal in 1996?

a	High Jump	b	Long Jump
c	Pole Vault	d	Triple Jump

7.29 Where did Jonathan Edwards break two world records in 1995?

a	Gothenburg	b	Oslo
c	Copenhagen	d	Malmo

7.30 In which subject did Jonathan Edwards graduate at Durham University?

a	History	b	Physics
c	Computing Science	d	Mathematics

7.31 What is the name of the Grand National winner, trained at stables in Brancepeth, Co. Durham in 2001?

a	Bindaree	b	Durham Edition
c	Tyneandthyneagain	d	Red Marauder

7.32 The Newcastle Falcons won the English Cup in which years?

a	2000 & 2003	b	2000 & 2004
c	2001 & 2004	d	1999 & 2003

7.33 What event, which began in 1904, claims to be Britain's oldest road race?

a	Scotswood Road pub race	b	Blaydon Race
c	Great North Run	d	Morpeth to Newcastle

7.34 What is the Northumberland Plate also known as?

a	Gosforth Silver Plate	b	Brandling Trophy
c	Beeswing Cup	d	Pit mans derby

7.35 What else, apart from Speedway, is held at Brough Park?

a	Cycling	b	Dog Racing
c	Athletics	d	Tiddlywinks

7.36 Who did Glen McCrory beat for the World CruiserWeight Championship in 1989?

a	Patrick Lumumba	b	Jeff Lampkin
c	Siza Makathini	d	Evander Holyfield

7.37 Where was this bout held?

a	Anfield Plain	b	Conset
c	Stanley	d	Tanfield

7.38 Which Co. Durham born athlete won a bronze in the marathon at the 1984 Olympics?

a	Mike McLeod	b	Peter Leggit
c	Paul Bainbridge	d	Charlie Spedding

7.39 Where, in 1974, did Brendan Foster break the world 3000m record?

a	Gateshead	b	Crystal Palace
c	Oslo	d	Paris

7.40 In 1956 an ice hockey team in Whitley Bay was formed. What was its name?

a	Whitley Warriors	b	Whitley Reivers
c	Whitley Bees	d	Whitley Sharks

7.41 Which South Shields born swimming Olympian broke the British and Commonwealth 100m breaststroke record in 2003?

a	Sam Foggo	b	Sue Rolph
c	Gavin Meadows	d	Chris Cook

7.42 Which of the following isn't/hasn't been a Northeast ice hockey team?

a	Billingham Bombers	b	Sunderland Chiefs
c	Crowtree Cheifs	d	Teesside Steelers

7.43 When was the first England Test match played at Chester-le-street?

a	2003	b	1995
c	1997	d	2000

7.44 Who were England's opponents at this game?

a	India	b	Zimbabwe
c	Pakistan	d	New Zealand

7.45 In which event did Chris Newton win a bronze medal at the 2000 Olympics?

a	1km Time Trial	b	Individual Pursuit
c	4000m Team Pursuit	d	Points Race

7.46 Who is a British Champion surfer from Newcastle?

a	Shaun Skilton	b	Sam Lamiroy
c	Lee Bartlett	d	Llewellyn Whittaker

7.47 The O'Neill Surfing British Cup has been held at which Northeast Beach?

a	Seaton Sluice	b	Druridge Bay
c	Whitley Bay	d	Tynemouth Longsands

7.48 How many minor counties championships did Durham C.C.C. win between 1900 and 1984?

a	9	b	15
c	7	d	5

7.49 Which team did not play at the Riverside in the Cricket World Cup in 1999?

a	Pakistan	b	Bangladesh
c	Scotland	d	South Africa

7.50 What is the name of the threatened athletics stadium in South Shields?

a	Simonside Green	b	Gypsies Green
c	Westoe Park	d	Harton Park

When I think of all the good
times that I've wasted, having
good times,
When I think of all the good
time that's been wasted,
having good times,
When I was drinkin',
I should've been thinkin'.
When I was fighting,
I could've done the right
thing.
All of that boozin',
I was really losin',
Good times'
Good times.

'Good Times', The Animals

8
Gannin Oot

'Are ye's doon the toon the neet?' is heard again and again as the masses pour out of St. James' Park on a Saturday afternoon. The fact that the Toon Army is already well tanked at this point doesn't matter, the Geordie passion for enjoyment probably cannot be surpassed, only equalled, in a few other parts of the UK.

Night time in Newcastle was Britain's best kept secret until recent years. Now, every bugger pours into the town at weekends, from all parts of the nation – something which is given a big Geordie welcome. Sitting in the pub opposite the Central Station on a Friday night you can watch for hours as groups of lads and lasses head over from their disembarkation point, have a quick pint while they find their bearings and then head off to their hotels and guesthouses. You can easily spot the visitors – they are the people out on the town with their coats on!

Booking a hotel room for a Saturday night is an almost impossible task. Newcastle bucks the usual trend by increasing its room occupancy rate at weekends. It wasn't that long ago that people didn't think of Newcastle as a destination but rather as a mad town that you passed *through* on the way to Edinburgh.

Drinking circuits change over the years, pubs become bars . . . then pubs again. Crawls change with industry. The legendary boozers of the Scotswood Road declined in numbers when the tens of thousands of hardy folk no longer worked in factories such as Armstrong's situated near there. Today, the remaining pubs form the crux of Newcastle's 'Gay Triangle' – how times change!

Geordies like to pub crawl, and we don't like to sit down. In Glasgow and London, for example, friends meet up and 'sit'. In the Northeast we stand, drink and then move on. If we haven't visited at least ten watering holes in one night then something has gone wrong, but since the next pub is usually next door, or across the road, it isn't far to walk! The term MVVD most certainly points to the Northeast – 'Male Vertical Volume Drinker'.

8.1 Which bar incorporates the replica of the Royal Arcade?

a	Stereo	b	Revolution
c	The Swan	d	Bar 55 degrees

8.2 Which Bigg Market pub used to be a Coaching Inn?

a	The Old George	b	Blackie Boy
c	Balambras	d	The Turks Head

8.3 The Hyena Comedy Café is located where in Newcastle?

a	The Quayside	b	Grey Street
c	The Cloth Market	d	The Haymarket

8.4 The Lord Collingwood in Clayton Street is also known by which other name?

a	Monkey Bar	b	Fish Bar
c	Crow Bar	d	Dog Bar

8.5 Which famous blues bar stood on Blenheim Street?

a	The Brown Bear	b	The Barking Dog
c	Fat Sams	d	The Broken Doll

8.6 Which hugely successful Northeast comedian opened the Talk of the Tyne club in Gateshead?

a	Billy Fane	b	Bobby Hooper
c	Bobby Pattinson	d	Billy Martin

8.7 Where do most people get 'stood up' in Newcastle?

a	Greys Monument	b	Central Station
c	Haymarket	d	Quayside

8.8 What beer was advertised to a well known Paul Young song?

a	Lorrimers Best Scotch	b	Newcastle Exhibition
c	Newcastle Brown Ale	d	McEwans Best Scotch

8.9 The Market Lane Pub is more commonly known as what?

a	The Clock Bar	b	The Monkey Bar
c	Trade Bar	d	The Fish Bar

8.10 Which famous rock venue/dance hall/music venue was where the Gate complex now stands?

a	The Mayfair	b	The Jubilee
c	The Haymarket	d	The Mecca

8.11 What was a previous name for the Newcastle club Ritzies?

a	Tuxedo Junction	b	Greys Club
c	Madison's	d	The Studio

8.12 Who is the proprietor of the Rupali restaurant?

a	Lord Bigg	b	Lord of Harpole
c	Lord Such	d	Lord Singh

8.13 Who brewed 'Double Maxim'?

a	Scottish & Newcastle	b	Cameron's
c	Vaux	d	Castle Eden

8.14 What is the long-standing nightclub in Stowell Street, Newcastle called?

a	Fat Sams	b	Rosie's
c	The Stage Door	d	The Studio

8.15 Which bar had moving heads behind the bar and a moving bicycle?

a	Offshore 44	b	The Marketplace
c	Rosie's Bar	d	The Red House

8.16 In what year did the Mayfair in Newcastle close?

a	1999	b	2000
c	1998	d	2001

8.17 Who were the last main act to play at the Mayfair?

a	Stuff Little Fingers	b	Reef
c	Echo and the Bunnymen	d	The Quireboys

8.18 Which pub near the Castle Keep is famous for its folk and political societies?

a	Crown Posada	b	The Lounge
c	The Archer	d	The Bridge Hotel

8.19 Which watering hole is located next to West Jesmond metro station?

a	The Lonsdale	b	Barras Arms
c	The Archer	d	The Station

8.20 Which pub/live music venue is well known in the Ouseburn Valley?

a	The Cluney	b	The Bridge
c	Cumberland Arms	d	Tap & Spile

8.21 What is the bar in the Newgate shopping arcade, famous for its pre-Newcastle United entertainment called?

a	Bourgognes	b	Blackett Arms
c	Idols	d	Rosie's

8.22 What fine Newcastle pub, in Dean Street, sports stained glass and navy hats?

a	The Tyne	b	The Baccus
c	Red House	d	The Crown Posada

8.23 Which rock bar is located behind Northumberland Street?

a	The Jubilee	b	The Princess
c	The Crown	d	Trillions

8.24 Before being a pub, what was the former function of The Union Rooms prior to it being derelict?

a	A department store	b	A gentlemens club
c	Trades Union HQ	d	Mining Institute

8.25 Which successful club was in Low Friar Street, Newcastle?

a	Empire Ballroom	b	La Dolce Vita
c	Oxford Galleries	d	Cavendish

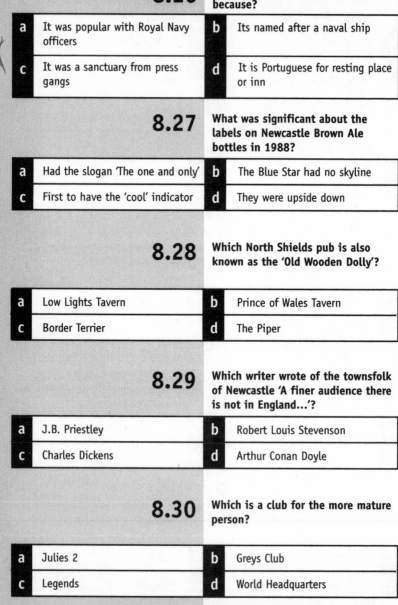

8.26 The Crown Posada is so named because?

a	It was popular with Royal Navy officers	b	Its named after a naval ship
c	It was a sanctuary from press gangs	d	It is Portuguese for resting place or inn

8.27 What was significant about the labels on Newcastle Brown Ale bottles in 1988?

a	Had the slogan 'The one and only'	b	The Blue Star had no skyline
c	First to have the 'cool' indicator	d	They were upside down

8.28 Which North Shields pub is also known as the 'Old Wooden Dolly'?

a	Low Lights Tavern	b	Prince of Wales Tavern
c	Border Terrier	d	The Piper

8.29 Which writer wrote of the townsfolk of Newcastle 'A finer audience there is not in England...'?

a	J.B. Priestley	b	Robert Louis Stevenson
c	Charles Dickens	d	Arthur Conan Doyle

8.30 Which is a club for the more mature person?

a	Julies 2	b	Greys Club
c	Legends	d	World Headquarters

8.31 Which massive Sunderland dance hall could easily accommodate 4000 dancers?

a	Palais de Dance	b	Wetherells
c	Seaburn Hall	d	The Rink

8.32 Which is an 'alternative' cinema with membership for £1 a year?

a	Tyneside Cinema	b	Whitley Bay Playhouse
c	The Gala, Durham	d	Side Cinema

8.33 Where will you find the Little Theatre?

a	Gateshead	b	Durham
c	South Shields	d	Haltwhistle

8.34 Which bar in Newcastle has rooms decorated from floor to ceiling in Burmantofts ceramic?

a	The Beehive	b	Centurion Bar
c	Forth Hotel	d	The Blackie Boy

8.35 Which glass-fronted bar is opposite The Baltic?

a	The Waterline	b	The Tyne
c	The Baltic Tavern	d	Picher & Piano

8.36 If you can't purchase a 'Borrel of Broon', what else might you buy instead?

a	Samson	b	Strongarm
c	Waggledance	d	Double Maxim

8.37 When 'The Boat' left Newcastle in 1989, which city did it go to?

a	Glasgow	b	Middlesbrough
c	Bristol	d	Liverpool

8.38 What was the original function of the Malmaison Hotel?

a	Bonded warehouse	b	Co-op warehouse
c	Ropery	d	Grain Store

8.39 For a famous beer brand, 'Florida is Orribler' than which Northeast town?

a	Sunderland	b	Newcastle
c	South Shields	d	Whitley Bay

8.40 Which singer did Newcastle Breweries commission to advertise Brown Ale for their first TV advertisements?

a	Owen Brannigan	b	Mike Elliot
c	Robert Allen	d	Graeme Danby

8.41 Complete the song lyric, 'Sitting in a sleazy snack bar sucking' what?

| a | sicky sausage rolls | b | a thumb |
| c | Devonshire slice | d | Slush Puppie |

8.42 Which is not a venue in The Gate complex?

| a | Tiger Tiger | b | Moodyblue Bar |
| c | Frankie & Benny's | d | Beyond Bar |

8.43 What does the pig blow in Newcastle's Bigg Market?

| a | A balloon | b | Wind |
| c | A whistle | d | Trombone |

8.44 Which was Newcastle's first multi-screen cinema?

| a | UGC | b | Odeon |
| c | ABC | d | Warner |

8.45 Which legendary club in Newcastle's Percy Street offered a residency to The Animals?

| a | The Mayfair | b | Mussel Inn |
| c | Club A Go Go | d | Curley's Bar |

8.46 Who brews L.C.L.?

a	Federation Brewery	**b**	Castle Eden
c	Greenalls	**d**	Scottish Courage

8.47 Which is the live music pub/venue under the Glasshouse Bridge?

a	The Cluny	**b**	The Tyne
c	Cumberland Arms	**d**	The Archer

8.48 Which of the following was a dance hall on the Westgate Road?

a	The Ramsgate	**b**	The Eastbourne
c	The Dover	**d**	The Brighton

8.49 Where in Newcastle would Dom Perignon 1959 be free flowing?

a	Pitcher & Piano	**b**	Red House
c	The Black Garter	**d**	The Apartment

8.50 In which bar near St James' Park will the clientele 'Drink Beer & Be Sincere'?

a	Strawberry	**b**	Three Bulls Heads
c	Trent House	**d**	The Black Bull

9

Works, Inventors & Scran

'I have this day dined upon fish, which probably dived upon the crews of several colliers lost in late gales.'

Lord Byron of Seaham

All that working and inventing is hungry work. That's why these topics are all lumped together in this chapter. Northumbria can boast a long and interesting history, but it was the Industrial Age which was responsible for many of the settlements and communities in the Northeast. In 1913, County Durham had 304 pits employing over 165,000 people; Sunderland was once the world's largest shipbuilding town and during World War II, produced more than a quarter of the nation's merchant and naval ship tonnage. This, along with the tonnage from the Tyne and Tees, indicates ship manufacturing of massive proportions.

In Wallsend it was joked that you knew the type of ships its yards were building by the colour of the town's front doors – whole streets painted battleship grey when Swan Hunter was building a naval vessel. Towns like Jarrow grew around a single employer. Charles Palmer developed a new sailing vessel, the first being *The John Bowes*. This ship was revolutionary in many ways and was the first steam-driven iron screw collier in the world. It had a double bottom to carry water ballast pumped out by her main engine prior to loading cargo and thus saved time and money. When Palmers Yard died, Jarrow died, with 80% unemployment in the town.

It is well known that today only a few large ships are launched in the River Tyne but its encouraging to learn that more than 50% of the 49er class vessels competing in the Athens Olympics were built at North Shields.

While some people worked in the factories, coal mines and ship yards, others were inventing. Like other areas in Britain moulded by the Industrial Revolution, the Northeast produced many creative, inventive people and some astounding engineers. The hilly terrain would prohibit canals and is one reason why the world's first passenger railway was established in the area. George Stephenson and his son Robert built many great structures around the world such as the Victoria Bridge in Montreal, the Royal Border Bridge at Berwick and railways such as the Manchester to Liverpool railway.

Many associate Geordie cuisine with pies, chips, mushy peas and gravy. Actually its pies, chips, salt, vinegar, mushy peas and gravy – we like them all. It's no surprise that one of the largest and most common UK high street brands which sell pies and pasties was established in Newcastle. More seriously, a growing tradition still prevails. Towns are littered with allotments and men still attend Leek clubs . . . down the local pub. Gardening book instructions like 'Leeks should be planted running from east to west ensuring the maximum amount of sunlight on their leaves enabling growth' would be added to with jealously guarded growing methods. Some growers would even camp outdoors, guarding their crops as the Leek Show date drew near.

9.1 Gladstone Adams from Whitley Bay patented what item in 1911?

a	Rifled naval gun	b	Windscreen wiper
c	Life jacket	d	Diving mask

9.2 Who merged railway departments with Stephenson's to form a larger locomotive company in 1937?

a	William Smith & Co.	b	Charles Palmer
c	Whitworth	d	Hawthorn Leslie

9.3 Whose massive works at Elswick once employed over 20,000 people?

a	Armstrong's	b	Mitchell's
c	Crowley's	d	Tennant and Allhusen's

9.4 Which famous Tyne-built liner held the Blue Riband award for crossing the Atlantic for 22 years?

a	R.M.S. Aurania	b	Turbinia
c	R.M.S. Ranpura	d	R.M.S. Mauratania

9.5 Who built this vessel?

a	Wallsend Slipway Company	b	Swan Hunter and Wigham Richardson
c	W.G.Armstrong, Mitchell & Co.	d	Clarke Chapman

9.6 What were known as 'White Cemeteries' by the people who worked in them?

a	Lead works	b	Munitions factories
c	Leather factories	d	Salt works

9.7 Who designed the *Turbinia*, the world's first steam turbine driven ship in 1894?

a	Charles Parsons	b	James Watt
c	William Chapman	d	William Clarke

9.8 Christopher Leyland, landowner, investor and skipper of the *Turbinia* lived where?

a	Dockendale Hall	b	Haggerston Castle
c	Deleval Hall	d	Styford Hall

9.9 Who invented the kipper at Seahouses in 1843?

a	Terry Kiln	b	Chas Archbold
c	John Woodger	d	Captain Craster

9.10 Which Alnwick hotel has a dining room fitted with fixtures salvaged from the *R.M.S. Olympic*, sister ship of *the Titanic*?

a	White Swan	b	Black Bull
c	Charlton House	d	Eider Duck

9.11 A flat bread is known locally as what?

a	A stottie	b	Oven bottom cake
c	A stovie	d	Pizza

9.12 What are 'Singing Hinnies'?

a	Fruit buns	b	A choir
c	Mince and dumplings	d	Girdle cakes

9.13 Which claims to be Newcastle's oldest Italian restaurant, established in 1965?

a	Ristorante Roma	b	The Godfather
c	The Italian Job	d	La Toscana

9.14 What wouldn't you find in Toon fast food outlets but would perhaps find in Sunderland?

a	Haggis	b	Parmies
c	Cheesy chips	d	Cheesy peas

9.15 From which vegetable is a Halloween lantern traditionally made from in the Northeast?

a	Pumpkin	b	Turnip
c	Potatoe	d	Marrow

9.16 What is the name for a local fishing vessel?

a	Schooner	b	Coble
c	Beamer	d	Collier

9.17 Where in Newcastle was Charles Parson's famous turbine works?

a	Benwell	b	Killingworth
c	Heaton	d	Walker

9.18 What was a popular soft drink not so long ago?

a	Dandelion and Burdock	b	Dandebeer
c	Dandeburd soda	d	Burdock beer

9.19 Which Northumbrian dish is made from onions and potatoes?

a	Cheviot Hash	b	Alnwick Hotpot
c	Pan Haggerty	d	Shepherds Lunch

9.20 From which Tyneside pit was 'firedamp' drawn by Sir Humphrey Davey for testing his Miners Safety Lamp?

a	Hebburn B Pit	b	Wardley Colliery
c	Follonsby Pit	d	Percy Main Colliery

9.21 During the First World War, what in Gateshead was manufactured by the 'Haggies Angels'?

a	Rope	b	Glass
c	Bread	d	Soap

9.22 According to the rhyme, how long is peas pudding in the pot?

a	1 week	b	9 days
c	6 hours	d	100 years

9.23 Where is the city farm?

a	Nuns Moor	b	Byker
c	Town Moor	d	Killingworth

9.24 Which footballer sampled the North Sea when buying a fishing boat, then famously remarked 'Sod that!'?

a	George Robledo	b	Mirandinha
c	Faustino Asprilla	d	Noberto Solano

9.25 Which narrow street in Newcastle was recently nicknamed 'Silicon Alley'?

a	Low Friar Street	b	Pink Lane
c	Broad Chare	d	Bath Lane

9.26 What did John William Hoggart of Gateshead invent?

a	Propeller	b	Polo mints
c	Wire rope	d	First flavoured potato crisps

9.27 What was 'Big Geordie'?

a	A wrestler	b	A mechanical digger
c	A ship	d	A mine shaft

9.28 Which Bigg Market curry house, featured in the *Guinness Book of Records*, serves the 'world's hottest curry'?

a	Vujon	b	The Rupali
c	Moti Mahal	d	Raj Tandoori

9.29 When the coal export industry was at its peak, roughly how many tonnes of coal were exported from the Tyne in one year?

a	55m	b	700,000
c	7.5m	d	23m

9.30 A packet of 'Rolos' would probably be made where in the Northeast?

a	Fawdon, Newcastle	b	Pallion, Sunderland
c	Newton Aycliffe	d	Peterlee

9.31 Which Newcastle-based baker now has over 1200 outlets?

a	Greggs	**b**	Milligans
c	Cathedral	**d**	Carricks

9.32 What was the nickname of the Newcastle bar that features at the start of the film *Get Carter*?

a	Robin Adair	**b**	Victoria & Comet
c	Long Bar	**d**	Trader Jacks

9.33 What first for Broon Ale happened in the year 2000?

a	First time on draught in Newcastle	**b**	Label lost the slogan "The one and only"
c	It outsold Budweiser in the USA	**d**	It was officially accepted in Sunderland

9.34 What is famously made in Meadomsly Road, Consett, Co. Durham?

a	Wine	**b**	Alpine dried food
c	Phileas Fogg snacks	**d**	Mint Cake

9.35 Which shipyard built and launched what's considered the world's first true oil tanker?

a	Armstrong, Mitchell & Co. Ltd	**b**	Sunderland Shipbuilding Co.
c	Swan Hunter	**d**	William Doxford & Son

9.36 What was the name of this vessel?

a	Gluckauf	b	Jahre Viking
c	Saxon Prince	d	Circassion Prince

9.37 What tank was manufactured at Vickers?

a	Crusader Tank	b	Competitor Tank
c	Panzar Tank	d	Chieftan Tank

9.38 Who demonstrated his light bulb at the Lit. and Phil on 3 February 1879?

a	Henricg Globel	b	Thomas Eddison
c	John Mawson	d	Joseph Swan

9.39 Referring to a well-known shop, which pie was sung about by the Toon Army at St James' Park?

a	Scotch Pie	b	Greggs Pie
c	Dickmans Pie	d	Mince Meat

9.40 In the song, what beverage was to be consumed with the pie?

a	Cup of Bovril	b	Chicken soup
c	Bottle of broon	d	Stewed tea

9.41 What breed of cattle was developed by the Colling brothers of Ketton Farm, Co. Durham?

a	The Durham Ox	b	Chillingham Cattle
c	The Dun Cow	d	Durham Heifer

9.42 Finish the slogan of locally produced flavoursome crisps, 'A canny bag o'' what?

a	Skips	b	Smiths
c	Walkers	d	Tudor

9.43 Where in Northumbria are famous kippers produced?

a	Craster	b	Boulmer
c	Amble	d	Seahouses

9.44 What family name has been producing these kippers for generations?

a	Charlton	b	Forster
c	Dodd	d	Robson

9.45 What is a famous Northumbrian drink made from honey?

a	Berwickshire Malt Whiskey	b	Lindisfarne Mead
c	Kielder Ale	d	Hartlepool Navy Rum

9.46 What traditional vessel is used to drink this?

a	Flagon	b	Horn
c	Flask	d	Mazer

9.47 What did the Castle Eden Beer revive recently after an absence of 30 years?

a	Castle Eden Ale	b	Nimmos XXXX
c	Castle Eden Bitter	d	East Durham Pale Ale

9.48 Which Tyneside brewery produces Prince Bishop Ale?

a	Big Lamp	b	Durham Brewery
c	Hadrian Brewey	d	Mordue Brewery

9.49 Which beer won Champion Beer of Britain in 1997 and is brewed by the Mordue Brewery?

a	Angel Beer	b	Workie Ticket
c	Geordie Pride	d	Radgie Gadgie

9.50 What often accompanies ham in sandwiches?

a	Peas pudding	b	Broon Ale
c	Pickle	d	Red sauce

10

Miscellaneous

'there is a special feeling of being a Geordie. If you go away you always want to come back.'

Alan Shearer

This section is a mixed bag of all the questions that didn't fit into the previous nine chapters. You will encounter everything from the Holy Jesus Hospital to the Jarrow Marchers to traffic-cone-wearing statues. You will also meet some of the Northeast's best-known exports: *Auf Weidersen Pet, The Likely Lads* and the ubiquitous Ant & Dec!

10.1 What creature is featured on the Newcastle coat of arms?

a	Unicorn	b	Fish
c	Lio	d	Sea horse

10.2 What was the name of the stricken ship from which Grace Darling and her father rescued survivers?

a	SS Forfarshire	b	SS Dumfriesshire
c	SS Ayrshire	d	SS Aberdeenshire

10.3 Who wrote the first ever *History of the English Peoples* in 776?

a	Cuthbert	b	Aiden
c	Oswald	d	Bede

10.4 Which Northumberland road is known as the 'Military Road'?

a	B6318	b	A69
c	A695	d	B6320

10.5 Which of the following towns is not twinned with Newcastle upon Tyne?

a	Gronigen, Holland	b	Newcastle, Australia
c	Nancy, France	d	Stavanger, Norway

10.6 Britain's oldest glassmaking industry was established where?

a	Byker	b	North Shields
c	Gateshead	d	Sunderland

10.7 What musical ensemble was formed in 1959?

a	Northern Soul	b	High Level Ranters
c	Northern Sinfonia	d	Opera North

10.8 What was the symbol of the Gateshead Garden Festival held in 1990?

a	Bridges	b	Butterfly
c	Sprig of Heather	d	Blue Bells

10.9 How many Jarrow Marchers are commonly perceived to have left for London?

a	100	b	200
c	3000	d	500

10.10 Whose statue on Westgate Road, Newcastle often has traffic cones on its head?

a	George Stephenson	b	Basil Hume
c	Richard Grainger	d	Joseph Cowen

10.11 Who in Newcastle, opposite the motorbike shops, fixed 'Everything from Zips to Bikini'?

a	Mr Pattel	b	Mr Rupi
c	Mr Raman	d	Mr Balani

10.12 The Holy Jesus Hospital, once the Joicey Museum also used to be what?

a	A sailors retreat	b	A soup kitchen
c	A school	d	A telephone exchange

10.13 According to local folklore, what was young Lambton deemed to kill once his heroic deed was done?

a	A goat	b	A sheep
c	The Sheriff	d	His father

10.14 Who played Jimmy Nail's sidekick in *Spender*?

a	Sammy Johnson	b	Tim Healy
c	Kenneth Norman	d	Berwick Kaler

10.15 Which northern earl inspired the naming of a London football team?

a	Lord Lucy	b	Lord Lambton
c	Duke of Westmoreland	d	Duke of Northumberland

10.16 Which Newcastle building used to house a cinema, Rockshots, Powerhouse and Laser Quest?

a	Alfred Wilson House	b	Carliol House
c	Cale Cross House	d	Milburn House

10.17 Where was the Spanish City?

a	South Shields	b	Roker
c	Cullercoats	d	Whitley Bay

10.18 Which band/singer has not performed at St James' Park?

a	Status Quo	b	Tina Turner
c	The Rolling Stones	d	Bruce Springsteen

10.19 In which year was the Laing opened?

a	1850	b	1875
c	1904	d	1936

10.20 What is grown in a trench?

a	Potatoes	b	Marrow
c	Turnip	d	Leek

10.21 Brian Johnson (AC/DC) formerly sang in which band?

| a | Busker | b | Geordie |
| c | The Animals | d | Dire Straits |

10.22 Which Swalwell man is said to have composed the tune more commonly known as 'Auld Lang Syne'?

| a | George Ridley | b | Major James Robertson |
| c | William Shield | d | Tommy Armstrong |

10.23 In Northeast galas, an instrument (usually all girl) jazz bands play is what?

| a | Kazoo | b | Trumpet |
| c | Trombone | d | Cornet |

10.24 Which famous suffragette is buried in the family grave at Morpeth?

| a | Emily Davison | b | Emmeline Pankhurst |
| c | Millicent Fawcett | d | Lydia Becker |

10.25 The line 'Half Church, Half Castle, 'gainst the Scot' was written about which Northeast place of worship?

| a | Hexham Abbey | b | Lindisfarne Castle |
| c | Norham Castle | d | Durham Cathedral |

10.26 Where in Newcastle were the first high rise dwelling places built?

a	Fenham	b	Shieldfield
c	Elswick	d	Byker

10.27 Apart from Central Station, where was the site of Newcastle's 'other' large station?

a	Fenham	b	Heaton
c	Jesmond	d	Mannors

10.28 Which Newcastle school was founded in 1545?

a	Royal Grammar School	b	Dame Allen's
c	The King's School	d	La Sagesse High School

10.29 Where was this originally located?

a	Jesmond	b	Near Blackfriars
c	Near St Nicholas Cathedral	d	Fenham

10.30 A tunnel connects the Ouseburn Valley to where?

a	Fenham	b	Spital Tounges
c	Gosforth	d	Heaton

10.31 Who hears the words 'Ahm a forst time caller anam abit norvous'?

| a | Alan Robson | b | The Samaritans |
| c | Tom Davies | d | Domino Pizza |

10.32 Every year Newcastle is presented with a Christmas tree from which city?

| a | Oslo | b | Stavanger |
| c | Bergen | d | Malmo |

10.33 Who was the modernist leader of Newcastle City Council in the 1960s?

| a | Peter Lee | b | Tony Flynn |
| c | Peter Henry Renwick | d | T. Dan Smith |

10.34 What is the tallest building in Newcastle?

| a | Shieldfield House | b | St James' Park |
| c | Vale House | d | Bewick Court |

10.35 By what other name is the Northumbrian Tartan known?

| a | Border Tartan | b | Shepherds Tartan |
| c | Reiver Tartan | d | Cheviot Tartan |

10.36 In what year was the 100th Durham Miners Gala?

a	1979	b	1986
c	1983	d	1991

10.37 Where is the Royal Northumberland Yacht Club?

a	Tynemouth	b	Berwick
c	Amble	d	Blyth

10.38 The Centre for Contemporary Art in Gateshead is known as what?

a	The Baltic	b	Prince Consort Building
c	T.C.A. (Tyne Contemporary Art)	d	Tate NorthEast

10.39 The statue to British Liberty is located in which stately grounds?

a	Cragside	b	Wallington Hall
c	Seaton Delaval Hall	d	Gibside Estate

10.40 What was Ant & Dec's first hit as PJ & Duncan?

a	'If I give you my number'	b	'Why me?'
c	'Lets get ready to rumble'	d	'Eternal love'

10.41 Which film did Sting star in, set in Newcastle, in 1988?

a	*Cul-de-sac*	b	*Nightclub*
c	*Happy Friday*	d	*Stormy Monday*

10.42 *Purely Belter* is a film adaptation of which book?

a	*Living in The Heed*	b	*The Season Ticket*
c	*Howay the Lads*	d	*The Bonny Lads*

10.43 *Gabriel and Me* starred which famous Scotsman?

a	Ewan McGregor	b	John Hannah
c	Sean Connery	d	Billy Connolly

10.44 *The Likely Lads* TV sitcom featured two characters, Terry Collier and who?

a	Tom Fenwick	b	James Bolam
c	Bob Ferris	d	Rodney Bewes

10.45 Who plays the character Neville Hope in *Auf Weidersen Pet*?

a	Jimmy Nail	b	Tim Healy
c	Kevin Whatley	d	Robson Green

10.46 To where did the Teesside Transporter Bridge go in the third series of *Auf Weidersen Pet*?

a	Arizona	b	Nevada
c	Cuba	d	Indiana

10.47 Who bought *Viz* in 1983?

a	Extremely astute people	b	John Brown Publishing
c	Newcastle Journal & Chronicle	d	The Mirror Group

10.48 In *Viz*, who are the 'Modern Parents'?

a	Malcolm and Cressida	b	Thomas and Lucinda
c	Tarquin and Guinevere	d	Dominic and Vanessa

10.49 Which character does not appear in any issue of *Viz*?

a	Black Bag	b	Mr Whicker
c	Big Vern	d	Blue Bottle

10.50 Which concert party troupe brought to the Spanish City earned the venue its name?

a	Toreadors	b	El Salvadors
c	Tartessos	d	Earlydors

THE ANSWERS

1 The River

1.1 How many bridges span the Tyne in Newcastle/Gateshead?
c   7

1.2 Robert Stephenson and T.E. Harrison built which bridge that spans the River Tyne?
c   High Level Bridge

1.3 Which river doesn't flow into the Tyne?
a   Old Nick Waters

1.4 A keelboat was crewed by a skipper, two keelmen and a boy. What was the boy known as?
a   A Pee Dee

1.5 Whose Oils stands on the banks of the Tyne in Gateshead?
d   Bretts

1.6 What is the most recently built Tyne river crossing?
a   Gateshead Millennium Bridge

1.7 Which burn flows through Jesmond Dene to the Tyne?
a   Ouseburn

1.8 Who was the engineer that built the Swing Bridge?
b   W.G. Armstrong

1.9 When did the Metro Centre, near the banks of the Tyne, in Gateshead open?
a   1987

1.10 How long is the River Tyne?
c   62miles

1.11 The largest vessel ever to sail along the River Tyne was called what?
c   *The Bonga*

1.12 A south pier built to stop the river silting at the mouth of the River Tyne is named what?
d   Groyne Pier

1.13 What was formed in Tynemouth in 1869?
a   First ever volunteer life brigade

1.14 What is the name of the floating nightclub moored near the Tyne Bridge?
a   Tuxedo Princess

1.15 What large monument can be seen overlooking the Tyne at Tynemouth?
d   Monument to Lord Collingwood

1.16 How long does it take for the Gateshead Millennium bridge to open or close?
b   4 mins

1.17 How high is the Tyne Bridge arch at its highest point?
a   55m

1.18 What was the BALTIC originally used as?
c   Flour mill

1.19 What was the name of the floating crane that brought the Gateshead Millennium Bridge up the Tyne to its present position?
d   *Asian Hercules II*

1.20 The meeting of the waters, the rivers North Tyne & South Tyne converge where?
a   Warden Rock

1.21 Which two communities are connected by the Tyne Pedestrian and Cycle tunnel?

c Howden & Jarrow

1.22 Which bygone riverside community would wear a blue jacket and yellow waistcoat?

a Keelmen

1.23 What is the name of the sculpture which hangs on the remains of the old Redheugh Bridge?

b *Once upon a Time*

1.24 Which riverside sculpture was originally commissioned for Gateshead at the Glasgow Garden Festival 1987?

c *Rolling Moon*

1.25 Where is the first River Tyne crossing point?

a Kingshaw Green

1.26 Which Aircraft Carrier was built at Swan Hunter, Walsend and launched in 1981?

c *HMS Ark Royal*

1.27 What famous Roman road travels through Co. Durham from Piercebridge to Corbridge?

a Dere Street

1.28 What transport link was opened on 19 October 1967?

b Tyne Tunnel

1.29 In which year was the massive wooden structure, the Dunston Staithes, completed?

b 1890

1.30 What was the last Navy frigate built by Swan Hunter?

d *HMS Richmond*

1.31 What, roughly, was the population of Gateshead in 1801?

a 8,500

1.32 What roughly was the population of Gateshead in 1901?

c 108,000

1.33 Which Tyne crossing, built in 1876, is in similar design, and a precursor to, the Tyne bridge?

a Hagg Bank Bridge

1.34 What happened on 6 October 1854?

a Great fire of Newcastle and Gateshead

1.35 Who founded St Pauls Monastery at Jarrow in the seventh century?

b Benedict Biscop

1.36 Who was the leader of the Tyne's most notorious press gang?

d Captain Bover

1.37 In the Discovery Museum, what is the largest ship model on display?

a *SS Serenia*

1.38 Where near the Tyne was the Roman fort Condercum?

a Benwell

1.39 How many Royal Navy vessels have borne the city of Newcastle's name?

d 8

1.40 Which port is not served by an International Ferry link from the Tyne?

d Hook of Holland

1.41 The River Tyne Improvement Act ending Newcastle's monopoly of the Tyne was passed by parliament in which year?

a 1850

1.42 What is the name of the latest Shields Ferry?

a *Pride of the Tyne*

1.43 What was the name of the ferry that this vessel replaced?

d *Freda Cunningham*

1.44 Where on the Tyne is the pumping station designed to take water from Kielder to the Tees?

a Riding Mill

1.45 In 1929, how many ferry routes operated between Newburn and the river mouth?

a 11

1.46 Which seventeenth-century gun battery guards the river Tyne?

a Clifford Fort

1.47 What is the world's largest square rigged sailing ship which visited the Tyne during the Tall Ships Race in 1993?

b *Sedov*

1.48 What is the smallest vessel of the Tyne Leisure Line fleet?

d *Island Scene*

1.49 The Tyne Bridge and Sydney Harbour Bridge were constructed by which engineering company?

a Dorman Long

1.50 What shipping hazard lies at the foot of the Tynemouth cliffs?

a Black Middens rocks

2 The Toon and Nearby

2.1 What is the Roman name for Newcastle upon Tyne, more specifically the fort and bridge?
c   Pons Aelius

2.2 By what other name has Newcastle been known?
d   Monkchester

2.3 What marked the border between Newcastle and the Bishops land on Newcastle's medieval bridge?
c   Blue Stone

2.4 Which Royal granted a charter to the town of Newcastle upon Tyne confirming possession of the Town Moor?
c   King Edward III

2.5 Which city in the U.S.A is linked with Newcastle upon Tyne?
d   Atlanta, Georgia

2.6 Which Newcastle street was allegedly the first street in the world to be lit by electricity?
a   Mosley Street

2.7 What colour is the 'carpet' in front of the Laing?
b   Blue

2.8 Which of the following is not a stair leading up from the Quayside?
d   Crooked Stairs

2.9 What is named after Earl Grey?
b   Tea

2.10 Which theatre in Newgate Street closed in 1963?
a   Empire Theatre

2.11 What was the department store at the corner of Market Street and Grainger Street?
a   Binns

2.12 Which famous watering hole in the Haymarket was demolished to make way for Bus station improvements and Marks & Spencer's extension?
d   Farmers Rest

2.13 What were public fountains in Newcastle/Gateshead called?
a   Pants

2.14 Which current Newcastle church, on the site of a large medieval church, was designed by David Stephenson?
c   All Saints

2.15 What was the name of the American clothes store that was off Westgate Road?
b   Flip

2.16 Which Arcade, built in 1832 and later demolished was reborn with a replica?
c   Royal Arcade

2.17 Where in Newcastle will you find a Marks and Spencer 'Original Penny Bazaar'?
d   The Grainger Market

2.18 The first department store in Newcastle was founded by which Weardale man?
a   Emerson Muschamp Bainbridge

2.19 Lord Armstrong donated which park to the city of Newcastle in 1883?

b Jesmond Dene

2.20 Where is the South African War Memorial?

c The Haymarket

2.21 In which store are there stairs with small, bent human figures supporting the handrail?

d Co-op

2.22 In which year did the Tall Ships Race first come to Newcastle?

a 1986

2.23 In which Newcastle museum would you find a mummy?

a Hancock

2.24 Where will you find Windows Music store?

b Central Arcade

2.25 Where does the more 'alternative' youth hang around on a Saturday afternoon?

c Old Eldon Square

2.26 What transportation point was opened on 26 July 1935 at a cost of £35,000?

d Newcastle Airport

2.27 Where did Stephenson build many of the world's first locomotives, including the *Rocket*?

c Forth Banks, Newcastle

2.28 Which building wasn't designed by John Dobson?

d Theatre Royal

2.29 What is Gateshead businessman John Barras famous for?

b Brewing

2.30 What used to be on the site of the Newburn Business Park?

a Power station

2.31 Which Newcastle street is well known for its many Chinese and Cantonese restaurants?

d Stowell Street

2.32 What was switched 'on' on 15 January 1959?

a Tyne Tees TV

2.33 Which section of the Metro was first to be opened in August 1980?

b Haymarket to Tynemouth

2.34 In the late thirteenth century, Newcastle was the leading English port for exporting which product?

d Leather

2.35 In which years were the Northeast Coast Exhibitions held?

c 1882 & 1929

2.36 The later Exhibition was held on part of the town moor. Where was the original Exhibition based?

b Tynemouth

2.37 The annual fair held at Newcastle, which is said to be Europe's largest non-permanent fair, is known as what?

d The Hoppings

2.38 Which community lived at Sandgate?

b Keelmen

2.39 Where in Newcastle was famous for its shoemakers and clog makers?

d Castle Stairs

2.40 Which building was designed by George Kenyon in the early 1950s?

b Civic Centre

2.41 Where was the grand Paramount Cinema opened in 1931?

c Pilgrim Street

2.42 Whose wife is buried in the cemetery of All Saints Church?

c George Orwell

2.43 Where in Newcastle would you find a stone rabbit with long teeth?

d St Nicholas Churchyard

2.44 Who designed The Guildhall in the Newcastle Quayside, opened in 1658?

a Robert Trollope

2.45 Trinity House, just off Broad Chare, was home to which Guild in 1505?

b Guild of Masters and Mariners

2.46 Where was Paddy's Saturday Market located in Newcastle?

c Milk Market

2.47 Who opened the third Redheugh Bridge in 1983?

d Diana, Princess of Wales

2.48 What was the former function, in 1895, of the Turnbull building, now converted to luxury apartments?

a Printing works

2.49 John Scott, lover of Bessie Surtees and a coal fitter's son, rose to become what in politics?

d Chancellor of England

2.50 Which Quayside building opened in 1877 is featured in a painting by L. S. Lowry hung in the Laing Art Gallery?

a Sailors Bethel

3 The Lingo

3.1 A sword with blunt edges used for performing is called a what?
d   Rapper

3.2 Home-made rugs made of cloth, often in mining villages in the area, are called what?
c   Clippy Mats

3.3 Other similar rugs made in the region are called what?
a   Proggy Mats

3.4 What is a spuggy?
a   Sparrow

3.5 A Mackem hails from where?
b   Sunderland

3.6 Locally, a latch on a door or gate is what?
d   Sneck

3.7 What is a skinch?
d   To call a truce

3.8 Where would you find a shuggyboat?
a   The Hoppings

3.9 Food can be known as what?
d   Scran

3.10 What is a Pit Yakkor?
c   Not a nice term to call someone

3.11 What is a nettie?
b   A lavatory

3.12 What is a local word for 'friend'?
b   Marra

3.13 A burn or beck in a steep valley flows through what?
d   A Dene

3.14 Where does a 'Smoggie' hail from?
c   Middlesbrough

3.15 To give someone a lift on a bike can be known as what?
b   A Croggy

3.16 What is 'Cannae be fashed'?
d   Opposite to enthusiastic

3.17 What does 'Haddaway an shite!' mean?
b   Never in the world

3.18 What is something if it 'knacks'?
b   Hurts

3.19 A boiler is what?
c   Is not pleasant to the eye

3.20 What is an oxter?
c   An armpit

3.21 If you have been 'plodgin', what have you been doing?
b   Paddling in the burn

3.22 If a boozer is described as being stowed it is what?
a   Full

3.23 What is 'Hoyinooteem'?
b   When the pubs close

3.24 What Geordie expression describes a rainy day?
c   Stottindoon

3.25 A baff weekend is what?
a   When you are skint

3.26 If a Geordie describes someone as 'Gitcanneyasoot' they are what?
b   Very pleasant

3.27 What is 'hoyintabs'?
a Throwing cigarettes

3.28 Where does the local word 'Gadgie' originate?
c Romany

3.29 Where would you buy 'kets'?
b Sweet shop

3.30 What is a 'jumper'?
a Ganzie

3.31 What is a 'workie ticket'?
d An aggravating person

3.32 What is a schooner?
b Summink tae drink broon in

3.33 In local folklore, what is a 'worm'?
a A dragon

3.34 What could be known as a 'Jamie'?
d Sunderland collier

3.35 A Sand-dancer hails from where?
b South Shields

3.36 In Geordie, what is a 'norse'?
c Trained medical staff

3.37 What is a 'liggie'?
b A marble

3.38 What other word is sometimes used?
b Penker

3.39 What in Northumberland and Durham is a 'Linn'?
c Waterfall

3.40 What is Geordie for 'Of course!'?
d Whey Aye!

3.41 Where would you find a Monkey Hanger?
b In Hartlepool

3.42 'Wor drums' are what?
a Are our instruments

3.43 What is 'Bountie'?
c Expression for 'its bound to'

3.44 A 'tap on' is what?
a Is when you get lucky

3.45 What is a 'radgie gadgie'?
d An angry man

3.46 'Had on man' means what?
a Please wait

3.47 What is a 'forkeytail'?
c An earwig

3.48 'He's champion he is' means what?
c That person is nice

3.49 'Would you like a cake or a meringue' would warrant a reply like what?
d Yes, you are correct, a cake please

3.50 Complete the sentence, 'A bogey....'
b has wheels

4 Yonks Back

4.1 The son of William the Conqueror started the building which is now the present–day Castle Keep. What was he called?

a Robert Curthose

4.2 What is the barbican added to the 'New Castle' around 1250 called?

d The Black Gate

4.3 Newcastle became a city when the Diocese of Newcastle was formed from the Diocese of Durham. Which year was this?

c 1882

4.4 Which king was prisoner in Newcastle for ten months in 1646?

b King Charles I

4.5 What was a former name for Bamburgh?

d Din Guyardi

4.6 Which great scholar lived in the Monasteries of Monkwearmouth and Jarrow?

c Bede

4.7 In which year was Gateshead annexed for two years to Newcastle?

b 1553

4.8 Which regiment raised 51 battalions during the great war, more than any other?

b The Northumberland Fusiliers

4.9 What is the Monastery at Jarrow called?

d St Pauls

4.10 What were the Roman fort remains located at modern day South Shields called?

a Arbeia

4.11 By what other name was Hadrian's Wall known?

b Pictish Wall

4.12 How long in modern miles is Hadrian's Wall?

b 73

4.13 Which town was home to Tyneside's fishwives?

a Cullercoates

4.14 The north's *Doomsday Book* is called what?

c *The Boldon Book*

4.15 Which town was known as 'Little Moscow' in the 1920s?

b Chopwell

4.16 Which Tyneside town had, at the height of its trade, over 200 salt pans?

c South Shields

4.17 The region's first colliery railways were known as what?

a Newcastle Roads

4.18 Which railway claims to be the world's oldest existing railway?

d The Tanfield Railway

4.19 Who founded the monastery at Lindisfarne?

b Aiden

4.20 What treasure dedicated to St Cuthbert is now kept at the British Library London?

a *The Lindisfarne Gospels*

4.21 In which year was this treasure taken from the Cathedral at Durham?

c 1539

4.22 Which Celtic tribe settled around the Tyne and nearby?

d Brigantes

4.23 What was the name of the Angle Kingdom north of the River Tees?

d Bernicia

4.24 What Celtic river name means 'Oak River'?

a Derwent

4.25 People in Co. Durham were sometimes known as what?

d Haliwerfolk

4.26 Which unpopular Bishop of Durham was slain at Gateshead in 1081?

c Bishop William Walcher of Loraine

4.27 Where in Newcastle were the Northumberland Assizes once kept?

a The Moot Hall

4.28 What Tyneside village was the site of a Civil War battle in 1644?

b Newburn on Tyne

4.29 Which castle is known as the Windsor of the North?

c Alnwick

4.30 In which year was Saltwell Park opened?

d 1876

4.31 William Wailes, who built Saltwell Towers, was famous for what?

b Stained glass

4.32 Where did sword makers from Soligen, Germany settle around the year 1690?

b Shotley Bridge

4.33 Which Northumbrian king founded the monastery at Tynemouth in 637?

d Oswald

4.34 Which Scottish king is buried at Tynemouth Monastery?

c Malcolm Canmore

4.35 What is the name of the old beacon, between Wreckenton and Windy Nook?

b Beacon Lough

4.36 By what other Northeast name is the Eider Duck known as?

b Cuddy Duck

4.37 Which Newcastle building houses The North of England Institute of Mining and Mechanical Engineers?

b Neville Hall

4.38 Who, in 1831, objected to Gateshead being represented in Parliament?

a Marquis of Londonderry

4.39 William Hedley is best remembered for two engines. Puffing Billy was one, what was the other?

c   Wylam Dilly

4.40 Which newspaper is now the UK's oldest provincial evening newspaper?

a   *South Shields Gazette*

4.41 Which Northumbrian king perhaps inspired the name of the city of Edinburgh?

c   Edwin

4.42 Which famous tea company, with premises in many Northeast towns, established a head office in Byker in 1926?

b   Ringtons Tea

4.43 From where to where, did Stephenson's Locomotives operate the world's first passenger railway?

a   Shildon to Stockton

4.44 The first lighthouse in the world to be powered by electricity is at Whitburn. What is it called?

c   Souter Lighthouse

4.45 What is the world's oldest railway bridge?

a   Causey Arch

4.46 Who is Northumberland's, and Britain's, most famous landscape gardener?

b   Lancelot 'Capability' Brown

4.47 Which battle probably established the Tweed as the border between Northumberland and Scotland, rather than Edinburgh?

c   Carham (1018)

4.48 Which battle is known in ballads as the Battle of Chevy Chase?

d   Otterburn (1388)

4.49 The Northumbrian flag is based upon whose banner?

a   St Oswald

4.50 Which Northeast coastal town is said to still be at war with Russia?

b   Berwick

5 Cultcha An Tha

5.1 Who wrote the famous Tyneside song 'The Blaydon Races'?
c Geordie Ridley

5.2 Who is the big and bonnie lass who likes beer?
b Cushie Butterfield

5.3 Which poet, born at Battle Hill, Hexham, wrote a volume of war poetry entitled *Battle*?
d Wilfrid Gibson

5.4 Which North Shields author wrote *The Machine Gunners* and *Fathom Five*?
a Robert Westall

5.5 Which Newcastle Theatre housed playwrights Lee Hall, Julia Darling and Alan Plater?
b Live Theatre

5.6 What is the founding name of the Newcastle People's Theatre?
a Clarion Dramatic Club

5.7 Which famous dramatist and socialist performed and made his last public speech at The People's Theatre?
a George Bernard Shaw

5.8 In the Blaydon Races, which bridge was crossed when the bus headed into Blaydon Town?
c Chain Bridge

5.9 A statue of whom stands in North Shields?
d Stan Laurel

5.10 The 'little waster' was more commonly known as what?
c Bobby Thompson

5.11 Which singer and songwriter with the band Lindisfarne died in 1999?
c Alan Hull

5.12 What is the local folk song commemorating a railway journey from Rowland's Gill called?
a 'Wor Nanny's a Mazer'

5.13 Paddy McAloon from Witton Gilbert founded which popular band?
a Prefab Sprout

5.14 To which country did Lambton go to in folklore and the song 'The Lambton Worm'?
c Palestine

5.15 Which 1960s Newcastle band was formed by Alan Price?
c The Animals

5.16 Which Beatles song was written in a Newcastle hotel and went on to become a massive selling disc?
b 'She Loves You'

5.17 Which hotel was this?
a Imperial Hotel

5.18 What folk organisation is based at the new Sage music centre in Gateshead?
b Folkworks

5.19 What children's TV entertainment programme was based in Tynemouth in the 1980s?
d *Supergran*

5.20 Which feature film staring Michael Caine was shot in and around Newcastle in 1971?
a *Get Carter*

5.21 Who was the author of the book which inspired this film?
d Ted Lewis

5.22 What's the name of the film set in Newcastle that stars Patsy Kensit?
c *The One and Only*

5.23 Cecil McGivern introduced which programme to regional BBC radio?
b *Wot Cheor Geordie*

5.24 Which Co. Durham born author writes the children's Horrible Histories?
d Terry Deary

5.25 Which Northumberland village celebrates New Year with a procession of flaming tar barrels?
c Allendale Town

5.26 Who did the BBC poach from Tyne Tees in 1964?
d Mike Neville

5.27 Who was the cousin of Cushie Butterfield?
b Tom Gray

5.28 What is the third fish that Little Jacky will have when the boat comes in?
c Mackerel

5.29 In what year did the Newcastle City Hall open?
a 1927

5.30 What was the first book to be published by Catherine Cookson?
c *Kate Hannigan*

5.31 Which famous engraver had workshops behind St Nicholas Cathedral and was a master and business partner of Thomas Bewick?
d Ralph Beilby

5.32 What was the first story to be published by Sidney Chaplin, while he was working as a miner in Co. Durham?
c *The Leaping Lad*

5.33 Which town is the current home of the Northumbrian Bagpipe Museum?
b Morpeth

5.34 Which song did Robson Green and Jerome Flynn reach No. 1 with in the UK singles charts?
d 'Unchained Melody'

5.35 Who was perhaps the most famous Northumbrian poet of the nineteenth century?
a Algernon Swinburne

5.36 Which of the Romantic painters was born in Haydon Bridge?
b John Martin

5.37 In which Shakespeare play does the Earl of Northumberland, Harry Hotspur appear in a major role?
b *Henry IV Part 1*

5.38 Which Mercury Music nominee based in Newcastle had a debut album called *Dog Leap Stairs*?

c   Kathryn Williams

5.39 Who wrote the music for 'Close The Coalhouse Door'?

c   Alex Glasgow

5.40 Which famous American maritime painter lived for nearly two years in Cullercoats?

a   Winslow Homer

5.41 Who stars as Kate Tyler in Eastenders?

d   Jill Halfpenny

5.42 Which famous film director was born in South Shields in 1937?

d   Ridley Scott

5.43 Who was a famous and popular Polish dwarf entertainer, 3ft 3ins high, who loved Durham and retired there in 1791?

a   Joseph Boruwlaski

5.44 Which Gosforth–born actor read electrical engineering at Newcastle University?

b   Rowan Atkinson

5.45 Which songwriter composed music for the stage show of *Billy Elliot*?

c   Sir Elton John

5.46 Who produced *Roger's Profanisaurus*?

d   Roger Mellie

5.47 Who has silver buckles on his knee?

b   Bobby Shaftoe

5.48 Which sculptor created *The Angel of the North*?

b   Anthony Gormley

5.49 Which popular music show in the 1980s was filmed at the Newcastle Tyne Tees television studios?

c   *The Tube*

5.50 Where is the home of Northern Stage?

a   Newcastle Playhouse

6 Footie

6.1 The highest league position attained by South Shields FC was sixth in the old second division. What season was this?

b 1921–1922

6.2 From which team did Newcastle sign Mirandinha?

a Palmeiras

6.3 Which County Durham club won the 'World Cup' in 1909 and 1911?

b West Auckland

6.4 Which team did they beat?

d Juventus

6.5 In which year was the Northern League formed?

a 1889

6.6 Who won the first Northern League championship?

a St Augustine's Darlington

6.7 Blyth Spartans played in the FA Cup 5th round replay in 1978 against which team?

b Wrexham

6.8 Who did Gateshead AFC beat in the FA Cup 3rd round in 1953 before reaching the quarter-final stage?

b Liverpool

6.9 What is the nickname of Berwick Rangers FC?

c The Borderers

6.10 A good Sunderland AFC team in the early 1900s were known as what?

b Team of all Talents

6.11 Which three years in the 1950s did Newcastle United win the FA Cup?

b 1951, 1952, 1955

6.12 Where was Sunderland AFC's first football ground?

d Blue House Field, Hendon

6.13 In what year did Newcastle United claim their first FA cup victory?

b 1910

6.14 Who was Newcastle's first 'manager'?

c Andy Cunningham

6.15 Who was the opposition in Newcastle United's first FA Cup victory?

c Barnsley

6.16 Which team did Newcastle United play when they recorded their highest attendance of 68,386?

c Chelsea

6.17 Newcastle United's record league victory was against Newport County in 1946. What was the score?

d 13-0

6.18 For Newcastle United, who holds the record of most league and cup goals in one season?

d Andy Cole

6.19 When Newcastle United beat Royal Antwerp in the UEFA cup in 1994 what was the aggregate score?

d 10-2

6.20 On 23 October 1986, which other team played at 'home' at Hartlepool's Victoria ground?

a Middlesbrough

6.21 Who was the Newcastle United captain who lifted the Inter City Fairs cup in 1969?

a Bobby Moncur

6.22 Which team did Newcastle United beat in the semi-final of their Fairs Cup run in 1969?

d Glasgow Rangers

6.23 Which goalkeeper of the Fairs Cup winning team of 1969 went on to manage the club in later years?

c Willie McFaul

6.24 Who did Newcastle United draw in the 5th round of their 1973/1974 FA Cup run?

a West Bromwich Albion

6.25 In the 1966 World Cup, which team did not play at Ayresome Park?

a South Korea

6.26 Who gives himself credit for the breaking of Newcastle's London Hoodoo in 2001?

d Uri Geller

6.27 What was a previous nickname of Sunderland FC?

a The Rokerites

6.28 In which year did Middlesbrough FC win the FA Cup?

They have never won the FA cup

6.29 Who were Darlington's first opponents when they reached the 2nd division for the first time?

a Nottingham Forrest

6.30 Which Northeast football team doesn't play in black and white stripes?

c Billingham Synthonia

6.31 In 1908 Sunderland beat Newcastle 9-1. What else happened that season?

b Newcastle won the league

6.32 How many times were Gateshead put up for re-election before losing their place in the Football League?

a 1

6.33 On 18 April 1903 Sunderland won a league match against Middlesbrough, what was unique about the game?

a Game was at St James' Park

6.34 Who were Newcastle United's opponents for Len Shackleton's debut?

c Newport County

6.35 How many goals did he score?

c 6

6.36 Who did Newcastle United play in the 6-6 thriller ZDS Cup tie in 1991?

b Tranmere Rovers

6.37 What colour star is Seaham?

b Red

6.38 Which past Newcastle United player 'Gets the ball, and scores a goal'?

d Andy Cole

6.39 Which successful Sunderland manager in the 1890s later moved on to establish Liverpool as a force?

c Tom Watson

6.40 Sunderland Football Club enjoyed top flight football from 1890 till which year?

a 1958

6.41 Where do Carlisle United play?

d Brunton Park

6.42 What was the name of the 'World' cup that West Auckland won twice?

a Sir Thomas Lipton Cup

6.43 Who was known as 'Mr Newcastle'?

b Stan Seymour

6.44 Who were the last team to visit Ayresome Park in a competitive game?

c Luton Town

6.45 Which famous football stadium architect designed stands at Roker Park?

d Archibald Leitch

6.46 When St James' Park lost out as a venue for the 1966 World Cup, which ground hosted the stage matches instead?

a Ayresome Park

6.47 Who scored the vital goal at St James' Park against Portsmouth at the end of the 1991/1992 season?

c David Kelly

6.48 Which team stopped Newcastle United's record unbeaten run at the start of the 1992/1993 promotion season?

a Grimsby Town

6.49 Which team did not play at St James' Park in Euro '96?

d Belgium

6.50 In Newcastle United's first Champions League campaign, which team was not part of the group?

b Croatia Zagreb

7 Other Sport

7.1 What was the previous name of The Newcastle Falcons Rugby Club?
a Gosforth

7.2 What were the original colours of the above team?
d Green and white hoops

7.3 In which ground do the rugby team play?
c Kingston Park

7.4 What was the name of the Newcastle Arena's first ice hockey team?
d Newcastle Warriors

7.5 In which year did Gosforth first win the John Player cup?
c 1976

7.6 What annual sport was re-instated in Newcastle in 1997?
b Rowing

7.7 From which team did the Newcastle Cobras originate?
a Durham Wasps

7.8 Which famous and successful boat was built by Harry Clasper?
b *The Lord Ravensworth*

7.9 In what year did Harry Clasper compete in his last rowing race?
c 1867

7.10 In what year was the inaugural Tyne Regatta?
b 1840

7.11 How many gold medals at Commonwealth, World and European games has Steve Cram won during his career?
a 6

7.12 Where was Tyneside's first ever dirt track race, later to become Speedway?
d Hillheads, Whitley Bay

7.13 What was formed on 4 June 1892 in the Lockharts Cocoa Rooms, Clayton Street, Newcastle?
b Newcastle United Workmen's Golf Club

7.14 What is the capacity for sport in the Newcastle Arena?
a 5500

7.15 What was the name of Gateshead's professional Rugby League side awarded a franchise in 1999?
c Thunder

7.16 Which Rugby League side bought the Gateshead outfit after just one season?
d Hull Sharks

7.17 Which team did England play in Jonny Wilkinson's debut in April 1988?
c Ireland

7.18 Which is the region's oldest and the UK's fourth oldest golf club?
a Alnmouth

7.19 Who established the Great North Run?
c Brendan Foster

7.20 In which year did Durham C.C.C. gain first class cricket?

d 1991

7.21 Which of the following was not a famous Tyne oarsman of the nineteenth century?

d Robert Coombes

7.22 In which event did Steve Cram compete and win a Silver medal in in the 1984 Olympics?

b 1500m

7.23 Which club did Brendan Foster and Steve Cram both compete for?

b Gateshead Harriers

7.24 What event did Brendan Foster compete and win a bronze medal in, in the 1976 Olympics?

d 10000m

7.25 Which is the Northeast's oldest established athletics club?

d Elswick

7.26 From which Northeast town is Chris Newton, bronze Olympian and Great Britain cycling team member from?

b Stockton on Tees

7.27 What is the motor racing venue just south of Darlington?

c Croft

7.28 In which event did Olympian Jonathan Edwards win a gold medal in 2000, and a silver medal in 1996?

d Triple Jump

7.29 Where did Jonathan Edwards break two world records in 1995?

a Gothenburg

7.30 In which subject did Jonathan Edwards graduate at Durham University?

b Physics

7.31 What is the name of the Grand National winner, trained at stables in Brancepeth, Co. Durham in 2001?

d Red Marauder

7.32 The Newcastle Falcons won the English Cup in which years?

c 2001 & 2004

7.33 What event, which began in 1904, claims to be Britain's oldest road race?

d Morpeth to Newcastle

7.34 What is the Northumberland Plate also known as?

d Pit mans derby

7.35 What else, apart from Speedway, is held at Brough Park?

b Dog Racing

7.36 Who did Glen McCrory beat for the World CruiserWeight Championship in 1989?

a Patrick Lumumba

7.37 Where was this bout held?

c Stanley

7.38 Which Co. Durham born athlete won a bronze in the marathon at the 1984 Olympics?

d Charlie Spedding

7.39 Where, in 1974, did Brendan Foster break the world 3000m record?

a   Gateshead

7.40 In 1956 an ice hockey team in Whitley Bay was formed. What was its name?

c   Whitley Bees

7.41 Which South Shields born swimming Olympian broke the British and Commonwealth 100m breaststroke record in 2003?

d   Chris Cook

7.42 Which of the following isn't/hasn't been a Northeast ice hockey team?

d   Teesside Steelers

7.43 When was the first England Test match played at Chester-le-street?

a   2003

7.44 Who were England's opponents at this game?

b   Zimbabwe

7.45 In which event did Chris Newton win a bronze medal at the 2000 Olympics?

c   4000m Team Pursuit

7.46 Who is a British Champion surfer from Newcastle?

b   Sam Lamiroy

7.47 The O'Neill Surfing British Cup has been held at which Northeast Beach?

d   Tynemouth Longsands

7.48 How many minor counties championships did Durham C.C.C. win between 1900 and 1984?

a   9

7.49 Which team did not play at the Riverside in the Cricket World Cup in 1999?

d   South Africa

7.50 What is the name of the threatened athletics stadium in South Shields?

b   Gypsies Green

8 Gannin Oot

8.1 Which bar incorporates the replica of the Royal Arcade?
d Bar 55 degrees

8.2 Which Bigg Market pub used to be a Coaching Inn?
a The Old George

8.3 The Hyena Comedy Café is located where in Newcastle?
d The Haymarket

8.4 The Lord Collingwood in Clayton Street is also known by which other name?
b Fish Bar

8.5 Which famous blues bar stood on Blenheim Street?
d The Broken Doll

8.6 Which hugely successful Northeast comedian opened the Talk of the Tyne club in Gateshead?
c Bobby Pattinson

8.7 Where do most people get 'stood up' in Newcastle?
a Greys Monument

8.8 What beer was advertised to a well known Paul Young song?
d McEwans Best Scotch

8.9 The Market Lane Pub is more commonly known as what?
b The Monkey Bar

8.10 Which famous rock venue/dance hall/music venue was where the Gate complex now stands?
a The Mayfair

8.11 What was a previous name for the Newcastle club Ritzies?
d The Studio

8.12 Who is the proprietor of the Rupali restaurant?
b Lord of Harpole

8.13 Who brewed 'Double Maxim'?
c Vaux

8.14 What is the long-standing nightclub in Stowell Street, Newcastle called?
c The Stage Door

8.15 Which bar had moving heads behind the bar and a moving bicycle?
c Rosie's Bar

8.16 In what year did the Mayfair in Newcastle close?
a 1999

8.17 Who were the last main act to play at the Mayfair?
b Reef

8.18 Which pub near the Castle Keep is famous for its folk and political societies?
d The Bridge Hotel

8.19 Which watering hole is located next to West Jesmond metro station?
a The Lonsdale

8.20 Which pub/live music venue is well known in the Ouseburn Valley?
a The Cluney

8.21 A bar in the Newgate shopping arcade, famous for its pre-Newcastle United entertainment called?
c   Idols

8.22 What fine Newcastle pub, in Dean Street, sports stained glass and navy hats?
d   The Crown Posada

8.23 Which rock bar is located behind Northumberland Street?
d   Trillions

8.24 Before being a pub, what was the former function of The Union Rooms prior to it being derelict?
b   A gentlemens club

8.25 Which successful club was in Low Friar Street, Newcastle?
b   La Dolce Vita

8.26 The Crown Posada is so named because?
d   It is Portuguese for resting place or inn

8.27 What was significant about the labels on Newcastle Brown Ale bottles in 1988?
d   They were upside down

8.28 Which North Shields pub is also known as the 'Old Wooden Dolly'?
b   Prince of Wales Tavern

8.29 Which writer wrote of the townsfolk of Newcastle 'A finer audience there is not in England...'?
c   Charles Dickens

8.30 Which is a club for the more mature person?
b   Greys Club

8.31 Which massive Sunderland dance hall could easily accommodate 4000 dancers?
d   The Rink

8.32 Which is an 'alternative' cinema with membership for £1 a year?
d   Side Cinema

8.33 Where will you find the Little Theatre?
a   Gateshead

8.34 Which bar in Newcastle has rooms decorated from floor to ceiling in Burmantofts ceramic?
b   Centurion Bar

8.35 Which glass-fronted bar is opposite The Baltic?
d   Picher & Piano

8.36 If you can't purchase a 'Borrel of Broon', what else might you buy instead?
d   Double Maxim

8.37 When 'The Boat' left Newcastle in 1989, which city did it go to?
a   Glasgow

8.38 What was the original function of the Malmaison Hotel?
b   Co-op warehouse

8.39 For a famous beer brand, 'Florida is Orribler' than which Northeast town?
d   Whitley Bay

8.40 Which singer did Newcastle Breweries commission to advertise Brown Ale for their first TV advertisements?

a   Owen Brannigan

8.41 Complete the song lyric, 'Sitting in a sleazy snack bar sucking' what?

a   sicky sausage rolls

8.42 Which is not a venue in The Gate complex?

b   Moodyblue Bar

8.43 What does the pig blow in Newcastle's Bigg Market?

c   A whistle

8.44 Which was Newcastle's first multi-screen cinema?

d   Warner

8.45 Which legendary club in Newcastle's Percy Street offered a residency to The Animals?

c   Club A Go Go

8.46 Who brews L.C.L.?

a   Federation Brewery

8.47 Which is the live music pub/venue under the Glasshouse Bridge?

b   The Tyne

8.48 Which of the following was a dance hall on the Westgate Road?

d   The Brighton

8.49 Where in Newcastle would Dom Perignon 1959 be free flowing?

d   The Apartment

8.50 In which bar near St James' Park will the clientele 'Drink Beer & Be Sincere'?

c   Trent House

9 Works, Inventors & Scran

9.1 Gladstone Adams from Whitley Bay patented what item in 1911?
b Windscreen wiper

9.2 Who merged railway departments with Stephenson's to form a larger locomotive company in 1937?
d Hawthorn Leslie

9.3 Whose massive works at Elswick once employed over 20,000 people?
a Armstrong's

9.4 Which famous Tyne-built liner held the Blue Riband award for crossing the Atlantic for 22 years?
d *R.M.S. Mauratania*

9.5 Who built this vessel?
b Swan Hunter and Wigham Richardson

9.6 What were known as 'White Cemeteries' by the people who worked in them?
a Lead works

9.7 Who designed the *Turbinia*, the world's first steam turbine driven ship in 1894?
a Charles Parsons

9.8 Christopher Leyland, landowner, investor and skipper of the *Turbinia* lived where?
b Haggerston Castle

9.9 Who invented the kipper at Seahouses in 1843?
c John Woodger

9.10 Which Alnwick hotel has a dining room fitted with fixtures salvaged from the *R.M.S. Olympic*, sister ship of *the Titanic*?
a White Swan

9.11 A flat bread is known locally as what?
a A stottie

9.12 What are 'Singing Hinnies'?
d Girdle cakes

9.13 Which claims to be Newcastle's oldest Italian restaurant, established in 1965?
a Ristorante Roma

9.14 What wouldn't you find in Toon fast food outlets but would perhaps find in Sunderland?
c Cheesy chips

9.15 From which vegetable is a Halloween lantern traditionally made from in the Northeast?
b Turnip

9.16 What is the name for a local fishing vessel?
b Coble

9.17 Where in Newcastle was Charles Parson's famous turbine works?
c Heaton

9.18 What was a popular soft drink not so long ago?
a Dandelion and Burdock

9.19 Which Northumbrian dish is made from onions and potatoes?
c Pan Haggerty

9.20 From which Tyneside pit was 'firedamp' drawn by Sir Humphrey Davey for testing his Miners Safety Lamp?

a   Hebburn B Pit

9.21 During the First World War, what in Gateshead was manufactured by the 'Haggies Angels'?

a   Rope

9.22 According to the rhyme, how long is peas pudding in the pot?

b   9 days

9.23 Where is the city farm?

b   Byker

9.24 Which footballer sampled the North Sea when buying a fishing boat, then famously remarked 'Sod that!'?

c   Faustino Asprilla

9.25 Which narrow street in Newcastle was recently nicknamed 'Silicon Alley'?

b   Pink Lane

9.26 What did John William Hoggart of Gateshead invent?

d   First flavoured potato crisps

9.27 What was 'Big Geordie'?

b   A mechanical digger

9.28 Which Bigg Market curry house, featured in the *Guinness Book of Records*, serves the 'world's hottest curry'?

b   The Rupali

9.29 When the coal export industry was at its peak, roughly how many tonnes of coal were exported from the Tyne in one year?

d   23m

9.30 A packet of 'Rolos' would probably be made where in the Northeast?

a   Fawdon, Newcastle

9.31 Which Newcastle–based baker now has over 1200 outlets?

a   Greggs

9.32 What was the nickname of the Newcastle bar that features at the start of the film *Get Carter*?

c   Long Bar

9.33 What first for Broon Ale happened in the year 2000?

a   First time on draught in Newcastle

9.34 What is famously made in Meadomsly Road, Consett, Co. Durham?

c   Phileas Fogg snacks

9.35 Which shipyard built and launched what's considered the world's first true oil tanker?

a   Armstrong, Mitchell & Co. Ltd

9.36 What was the name of this vessel?

a   *Gluckauf*

9.37 What tank was manufactured at Vickers?

d   Chieftan Tank

9.38 Who demonstrated his light bulb at the Lit. and Phil on 3 February 1879?

d Joseph Swan

9.39 Referring to a well-known shop, which pie was sung about by the Toon Army at St James' Park?

c Dickmans Pie

9.40 In the song, what beverage was to be consumed with the pie?

c Bottle of broon

9.41 What breed of cattle was developed by the Colling brothers of Ketton Farm, Co. Durham?

a The Durham Ox

9.42 Finish the slogan of locally produced flavoursome crisps, 'A canny bag o" what?

d Tudor

9.43 Where in Northumbria are famous kippers produced?

a Craster

9.44 What family name has been producing these kippers for generations?

d Robson

9.45 What is a famous Northumbrian drink made from honey?

b Lindisfarne Mead

9.46 What traditional vessel is used to drink this?

d Mazer

9.47 What did the Castle Eden Beer revive recently after an absence of 30 years?

b Nimmos XXXX

9.48 Which Tyneside brewery produces Prince Bishop Ale?

a Big Lamp

9.49 Which beer won Champion Beer of Britain in 1997 and is brewed by the Mordue Brewery?

b Workie Ticket

9.50 What often accompanies ham in sandwiches?

a Peas pudding

10 Miscellaneous

10.1 What creature is featured on the Newcastle coat of arms?

d   Sea horse

10.2 What was the name of the stricken ship from which Grace Darling and her father rescued survivers?

a   *SS Forfarshire*

10.3 Who wrote the first ever *History of the English Peoples* in 776?

d   Bede

10.4 Which Northumberland road is known as the 'Military Road'?

a   B6318

10.5 Which of the following towns is not twinned with Newcastle upon Tyne?

d   Stavanger, Norway

10.6 Britain's oldest glassmaking industry was established where?

d   Sunderland

10.7 What musical ensemble was formed in 1959?

c   Northern Sinfonia

10.8 What was the symbol of the Gateshead Garden Festival held in 1990?

b   Butterfly

10.9 How many Jarrow Marchers are commonly perceived to have left for London?

b   200

10.10 Whose statue on Westgate Road, Newcastle often has traffic cones on its head?

a   George Stephenson

10.11 Who in Newcastle, opposite the motorbike shops, fixed 'Everything from Zips to Bikini'?

c   Mr Raman

10.12 The Holy Jesus Hospital, once the Joicey Museum also used to be what?

b   A soup kitchen

10.13 According to local folklore, what was young Lambton deemed to kill once his heroic deed was done?

d   His father

10.14 Who played Jimmy Nail's sidekick in *Spender*?

a   Sammy Johnson

10.15 Which northern earl inspired the naming of a London football team?

d   Duke of Northumberland

10.16 Which Newcastle building used to house a cinema, Rockshots, Powerhouse and Laser Quest?

a   Alfred Wilson House

10.17 Where was the Spanish City?

d   Whitley Bay

10.18 Which band/singer has not performed at St James' Park?

b   Tina Turner

10.19 In which year was the Laing opened?

c   1904

10.20 What is grown in a trench?

d   Leek

10.21 Brian Johnson (AC/DC) formerly sang in which band?
b   Geordie

10.22 Which Swalwell man is said to have composed the tune more commonly known as 'Auld Lang Syne'?
c   William Shield

10.23 In Northeast galas, an instrument (usually all girl) jazz bands play is what?
a   Kazoo

10.24 Which famous suffragette is buried in the family grave at Morpeth?
a   Emily Davison

10.25 The line 'Half Church, Half Castle, 'gainst the Scot' was written about which Northeast place of worship?
d   Durham Cathedral

10.26 Where in Newcastle were the first high rise dwelling places built?
b   Shieldfield

10.27 Apart from Central Station, where was the site of Newcastle's 'other' large station?
d   Mannors

10.28 Which Newcastle school was founded in 1545?
a   Royal Grammar School

10.29 Where was this originally located?
c   Near St Nicholas Cathedral

10.30 A tunnel connects the Ouseburn Valley to where?
b   Spital Tounges

10.31 Who hears the words 'Ahm a forst time caller anam abit norvous'?
a   Alan Robson

10.32 Every year Newcastle is presented with a Christmas tree from which city?
c   Bergen

10.33 Who was the modernist leader of Newcastle City Council in the 1960s?
d   T. Dan Smith

10.34 What is the tallest building in Newcastle?
c   Vale House

10.35 By what other name is the Northumbrian Tartan known?
b   Shepherds Tartan

10.36 In what year was the 100th Durham Miners Gala?
c   1983

10.37 Where is the Royal Northumberland Yacht Club?
d   Blyth

10.38 The Centre for Contemporary Art in Gateshead is known as what?
a   The Baltic

10.39 The statue to British Liberty is located in which stately grounds?
d   Gibside Estate

10.40 What was Ant & Dec's first hit as PJ & Duncan?
c 'Lets get ready to rumble'

10.41 Which film did Sting star in, set in Newcastle, in 1988?
d *Stormy Monday*

10.42 *Purely Belter* is a film adaptation of which book?
b *The Season Ticket*

10.43 *Gabriel and Me* starred which famous Scotsman?
d Billy Connolly

10.44 *The Likely Lads* TV sitcom featured two characters, Terry Collier and who?
c Bob Ferris

10.45 Who plays the character Neville Hope in *Auf Weidersen Pet*?
c Kevin Whatley

10.46 To where did the Teesside Transporter Bridge go in the third series of *Auf Weidersen Pet*?
a Arizona

10.47 Who bought *Viz* in 1983?
b John Brown Publishing

10.48 In *Viz*, who are the 'Modern Parents'?
a Malcolm and Cressida

10.49 Which character does not appear in any issue of *Viz*?
d Blue Bottle

10.50 Which concert party troupe brought to the Spanish City earned the venue its name?
a Toreadors

HOW DID YOU DO?

Score	Verdict
500–480	You must have either the divine influence of St Cuthbert behind you or your pants seem to be on fire?
479–420	To twist the words of Billy Purvis, 'Thous a real Geordie!' Well done!
419–350	You know lots about Newcastle, Tyneside and the whole Northumbrian area. Well done.
349–220	Not bad. Room for improvement. Have some kippers washed down with a Borrel of broon for some extra inspiration.
219–50	Definite room for improvement. Not even a fine ham & peas pudding sarnie washed down with a case of Lindisfarne mead, while reading the latest *Viz* annual would help.
49–0	Did you enjoy your weekend break in the Northeast?